How To Repair Small Appliances

by

JACK DARR

HOWARD W. SAMS & CO., INC.
THE BOBBS-MERRILL CO., INC.
INDIANAPOLIS · KANSAS CITY · NEW YORK

FIRST EDITION

FOURTH PRINTING—1971

International Standard Book Number: 0-672-20524-6
Library of Congress Catalog Card Number: 61-10963

Contents

Preface

At first glance some appliances may seem complicated, but actually they are not. Taking an appliance apart is often tricky, but it can be done with a little know-how and patience. Once you learn how to replace a worn or broken line cord, install a defective heating element or thermostat, or replace motor brushes, you should have very little trouble in repairing most home appliances.

The purpose of this volume, along with its companion Volume 1, is to supply the information needed to repair and service electrically operated home appliances. Whether your interest in maintaining appliances is for your own benefit, as a profitable sideline, or as a full-time occupation, you will find the information required in this handy reference.

With the appearance on the market of a large number of complex-looking automatic and semiautomatic appliances, a greater amount of knowledge is required by the serviceman, dealer, and handyman in order to intelligently understand the construction and operation. It is important to be able to troubleshoot and repair an appliance with a minimum of effort. Resorting to time-consuming guesswork is costly in time and frequently exasperatingly ineffective.

The experience and knowledge behind the text on these pages will help you successfully bypass the guesswork, experimenting stages. Keep this volume and Volume 1 handy, refer to the text and illustrations, and you should find keeping home appliances working is not a very difficult task.

JACK DARR

1

Diagnosis of Trouble

On getting a complaint that a certain appliance is not working, the first thing we must do is to find out why. If we use a logical sequence of tests based on the knowledge of how the appliance works, we can find the trouble and fix it quickly. Random "poking around" can take a lot of time, and you'll find the trouble only by accident. The basic method of fixing any kind of electrical apparatus is to use the logical sequence method of testing. All machines are inherently logical, and if we don't use logic when working on them, we are wasting time. The logical sequence of tests for this kind of apparatus is to find out if there is any electrical power to the unit; we must have this before it can work at all. Second, we must find out just which part is not working, such as the motor, heating element, etc. Third, we must see if it can be fixed or if we will have to replace it. That's all there is to this method.

Find out the nature of the complaint—completely dead, works intermittently, makes funny noises, etc. From here, we can go on to testing one particular part and save a lot of time. For example, if the complaint is "rattles," we can skip one step in the procedure—if it rattles, it is at least trying to work and it does have power; we can skip the step that calls for checking the line cord, plug, etc. and start looking for loose screws or parts.

TESTING TECHNIQUES

Check the line cord for signs of bad insulation, and the plug for loose connections. If the appliance does not work, make sure that

7

the plug fits tightly in the wall outlet, and check to make sure that the outlet itself is working properly. A common trouble with line cords is a broken wire inside the insulation near the plug. Hold the plug with one hand and bend the wire back and forth; if the appliance suddenly starts to work, cut off the cord about 6 inches from the plug and install a new plug.

If the cord seems to be in operating condition, pull the plug, and open the case of the appliance so that you can get at the other end of the cord. If the ends are fastened with wirenuts, take these off. Make sure that the wires are not touching each other or any part of the appliance. Plug it in again, and check it with a light bulb between the exposed ends to make certain that you're getting power up to that point. If you do, then the cord is definitely in good shape, and the trouble is in the appliance itself.

Continuity

Every electrical circuit must have *continuity*, which means that the wires must not be broken. There must be a "continuous circuit" from one side of the a-c line, through the cord, switch, motor, heating element or any type of load, through the other side of the cord and back to the a-c line again, as shown in Fig. 1-1.

You can check the a-c circuit very quickly with one of the neon testers. For example, to check a switch, first check the a-c line voltage at the ends of the cord, between points A and B in Fig. 1-2. If the lamp glows, then turn the switch on, and check from points A to C. If it glows here, the switch is working, and the trouble is in the load. This is the process of logical elimination. Details of finding the troubles in the load will be given in the discussions of the various appliances.

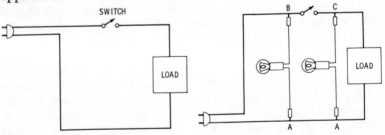

Fig. 1-1. A simple circuit illustrating the electrical-continuity path.

Fig. 1-2. A method of checking continuity or voltage.

SAFETY PRECAUTIONS

The power supply to your home is 117-volt, 60-cycle alternating current, and it can inflict serious injury or even death if you are careless. You must know how to handle it, what to do, and, above all, what *not* to do. Learn the rules and obey them at all times. Train yourself in safe working methods, and, most important, never get careless or contemptuous of electricity—this can be fatal. The professional electrician seems to handle electrical wires with carelessness, but this is not true. He is trained to take these safety precausions automatically.

There are a very few simple rules that you must follow:

1. *Never touch a bare wire* if the appliance is plugged into an electrical outlet. You can get a shock by touching the wires; the circuit is completed through your body. If you are wearing leather-soled shoes and standing on bare earth or a cement floor, you are grounded. The "service wires" from the transformer goes to your house load-center, where the circuit breakers protect your wiring against shorts. One side of the service line is always grounded, but the other side has 117 volts alternating current *with respect to ground* at all times. You can make voltage tests to find out which one is hot. However, when you are *working* on any kind of electrical equipment, be very sure that all power is *off*, by pulling the plug.

2. *Never* work on an appliance that is plugged in. You can make certain tests, as we said, but when you change parts, make connections, disconnect wiring, etc., make sure that the line plug is pulled out of the wall outlet and lying on the bench or table where you can see it.

3. For the safety of the one who will use this appliance, be *very* sure that there are no short circuits from the a-c wiring to the metal case of the appliance. Water pipes make a perfect ground; therefore if the metal case of a shorted toaster and the sink faucet are touched at the same time, a dangerous or fatal shock can be obtained.

When an appliance is disassembled, note very carefully how the wire connections are made, and be sure that they are put back so that there will never be any possibility of a bare wire getting in contact with any other part of the appliance. After completing the repairs, check for voltage between the case of the appliance and a water pipe. Pull the line plug, reverse it, and recheck. If your test lamp does not light in either position, it will indicate proper wiring of the line cord. There is always the chance of an accidental short or leakage between the internal wiring and the case. This can be an internal leakage in the motor windings, etc. It can be a "dead short" or just a leakage, which can cause the complaint of "it tingles whenever I touch it." Investigate this immediately; a "tingle" means a small leakage, but this can turn into a short circuit at any time.

Grounding of Appliances

Lately, some appliances have been using three-wire line cords with "polarized" plugs. These have the regular two flat prongs and a third round prong; these fit into a special wall outlet. The third (round) prong is an extra ground, and it is always connected to the frame of the appliance. If an internal short circuit should occur, it would simply blow the fuse or kick out the circuit breaker, but there would never be any dangerous voltage between the case of the appliance and ground. The three-prong plug may already be in use in your home, but, if not, it can be added at any time, if you want the protection.

Later on, you will be shown how to check for normal wear and aging of insulation, bad line cords, connections, etc. You can spot potential hazards and cure them before they become really dangerous. Make sure that you do not *add* any potential hazards while you are working on the appliance.

TOOLS AND TESTING

Any kind of repair job is easier if you have the right tools. To work on electrical appliances, you will not need a lot of expensive tools, but it will be much simpler if you have the right ones. You will find screws set down in holes, hard-to-get-at bolts, and such things. With the proper tool, they are simple to handle, but without it life can get complicated. You can find these tools at hardware stores, radio supply houses, and such places. Fig. 1-3 shows the essential tool kit: a 6-inch standard screwdriver, a *Phillips* screwdriver, a pair of 6-inch gas-pliers, a 4-inch adjustable wrench, and a pocketknife. With these tools you can take apart and reasssemble almost all common home appliances. Fig. 1-4 shows some helpful special tools; at the right is a set of nutdrivers or socket wrenches, from ⅛ inch up to ½ inch in steps of 1/32 inch. An extra handle is provided to give better grip on the small handles. Next to these are two screwholding type screwdrivers, very handy for getting screws and bolts started in tight places. At left is a three-way tap with a plastic handle, with the three most common sizes of thread. This is useful for restoring damaged threads in screw holes, or for threading oversize holes to the next larger size of screw.

Fig. 1-5 shows a handy tool; this is a *crimping tool*, with some samples of the terminals used. By using these terminals, you can put new connections on any wire without having to solder them. In some cases, this is essential; because you cannot solder terminals to

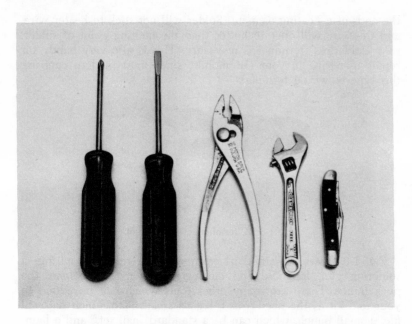

Fig. 1-3. The essential tools needed in appliance repair.

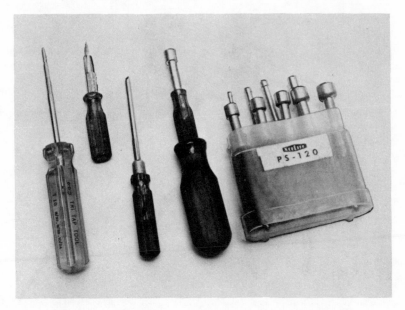

Fig. 1-4. Special tools used in making the repair job easier.

the ends of a heating element. Solder will not stick to heater wire, and the wire will operate hotter than the melting point of solder, so a "solderless" terminal is necessary. This is also very handy for repairing wiring in your automobile, since most modern cars use this type of wiring terminal.

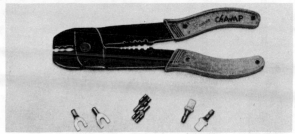

Fig. 1-5. A terminal crimping tool.

Fig. 1-6 shows the standard equipment for repairing wiring; a soldering gun, longnose and cutting pliers, and, of course, the pocketknife. There are many other tools which can be added to your tool kit as the need arises, e.g., a small 6- to 8-inch flat mill file, a small punch, which can be a standard "nail set," and a ham-

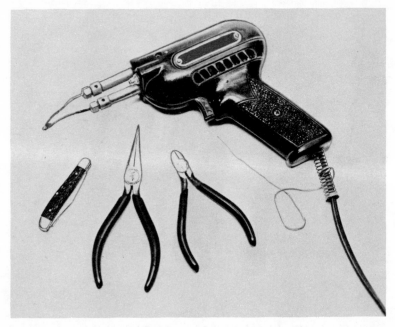

Fig. 1-6. Tools necessary for wire repair.

mer. You will find some appliances which have been riveted together. The only way to take these apart is to file off the head of the rivet and use a punch to knock it out. You can replace these by using "pop" rivets, also available at radio and auto supply stores. However, if you want to make the appliance easier to disassemble the next time, replace the rivets with No. 6 screws with nuts.

Use lockwashers under all nuts, and they will stay tight much longer. In cases where you cannot get to the inside of the unit to put on a nut, use a "self-tapping" or "metal screw." The metal screw cuts its own threads as it is installed, and it is found in a great many sheet-metal applications today. If one of the metal screws has been stripped out, use the next larger size; for instance, if the original screw was a No. 4, and it will not hold because the hole has been enlarged, use a No. 6 screw. The metal screws come with standard and *Phillips* heads, and in a great many applications (such as auto radios) they are hexagonal-head ¼-inch types. To get these out, you will need the ¼-inch nutdriver of the type shown in Fig. 1-4.

ELECTRICAL TESTING

We will need to check for electrical power in all appliances, and the simplest way to do this is to check for voltage. You can get small, imported, a-c voltmeters for less than $10.00 each, but many professional men use a simple "test lamp" which costs even less. Fig. 1-7 shows the two most common types of test lamps. At the top is an incandescent lamp in a weatherproof socket. The socket is covered with soft rubber and has flexible wire leads. Attach a pair of insulated test clips to these and put in a small 7-watt lamp, and you

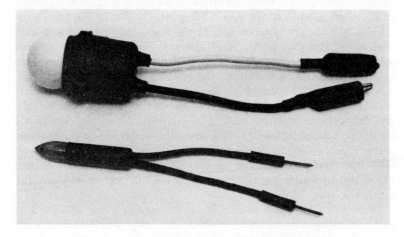

Fig. 1-7. Illustrating two common-type test lamps.

will be ready to go. To check for the presence of voltage across any circuit, just clip one lead to each side and, if the lamp lights, voltage is present.

Also shown is a special neon voltage-tester, sold in auto supply stores, radio stores, etc. A tiny neon bulb has a plastic housing and flexible leads with test tips. A series resistor is used inside the housing to make the lamp operate on 117 volts, or even on 220 volts for short periods. The lamp will glow on 117 volts, and glow much brighter

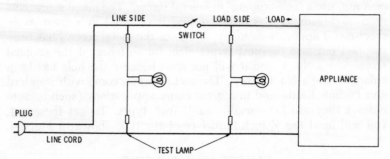

Fig. 1-8. Checking an appliance switch with a test lamp.

on 220 volts. There are advantages and disadvantages, as will be explained, but this type of test lamp is not expensive and should be included in your test equipment.

Using the Test Lamps

The 7-watt test lamp can be used for testing line cords, switches, and similar circuits. For example, if you want to check a line cord for a possible intermittent condition, hook the test lamp to the ends of the cord inside the appliance. Plug it in, and turn the switch on. The lamp should light. Now, hold the line cord and shake it back and forth. Move it, pull it, and watch the lamp. If there are any intermittent connections, the lamp will go off and on or flicker. To check a switch, hook the lamp from one side of the line to the "load" side of the switch (see Fig. 1-8) so that the current has to flow through the switch. If you wish, you can use a most useful electrical test here—the "simulated load." For example, if you are checking a small appliances (about 35–40 watts) disconnect the appliance and put a 50-watt lamp in the tester. By hooking this across the line, you will draw the same amount of current as the appliance. You can check this by looking at the rating-plate on the case; it will give the normal wattage drawn.

Now turn the switch on and see if it operates every time. If it is dirty or making intermittent contact, the lamp will flicker or even refuse to light at all. The neon tester can be used for this, but, because of its sensitivity, it is not as reliable as the load test. Even if the switch is dirty, the neon lamp will light, because it draws very little current. You can use this test for loads up to about 150 watts. For large heating-element appliances, such as space heaters, etc., which can pull up to 1000 watts, it is not practical. The best way is to use the heating element itself as the load.

The sensitivity of the neon tester can be put to good use. For example, to find out whether a certain circuit is grounded or not, hold one of the test tips in your hand, and touch the *other one* to the circuit. If there is any voltage present, the lamp will glow. The current here passes through your body, but it is so very small that you cannot feel it. This test is especially useful when one is working on house wiring, if you check both sides of the line and do not get a glow, then there is no voltage. The small tips of the test leads can be used to find out if there is any voltage at a wall outlet. Push them into the slots, and if there is voltage present, the lamp will light up brightly. If you get no light on this test, then check the fuses or circuit breaker. You must have voltage at the outlet before you can make any further tests.

Another "dirty switch" test can be made with the neon lamp. Plug in the appliance, turn it *on*, and then touch the test tips directly across the switch itself. Of course, when the switch is turned *on*, it should be a complete "short circuit." However, if it is dirty or not making contact properly, there will be a small voltage drop across the switch. If the lamp flickers when across a closed (on) switch, the switch is probably very dirty and should be replaced.

Testing for Grounds

As we said, there is one very important test that must be made on *all* appliances when you finish the repair. This is to find out if the case of the unit is shorted to the a-c line. If you have been careful, this will not happen, but never take chances with electricity—find out by making positive checks. Plug in the appliance and turn it on, and then touch one side of the little neon tester to the case. Hook a long piece of wire to a grounded object, and touch the other tip of the neon tester to this, keeping both hands clear. If you have a ground inside the case, the lamp will glow.

If it passes this test, pull the plug, turn it halfway over and put it back. Now repeat the test. Remember, we said that one side of the a-c line is hot at all times and the other is always grounded. So this second test will catch any kind of one-sided ground that might be present. Incidentally, on larger appliances, such as the washer, drier, etc., you can make it perfectly safe by running an *extra* ground wire from the frame of the unit to a water pipe. Fasten one end of the ground wire to a bolt, and clamp the other to the coldwater pipe. If the unit does short out, you will blow the fuse but no one will be injured.

SWITCH CLEANING AND REPLACEMENT

Switches are one of the most common causes of appliance trouble. In many appliances they are the only moving part. As a switch is used, its contacts gradually get dirty or burned from arcing. Eventually the time comes when the contacts simply will not close. The tests previously given will show this. If the switch is intermittent, it can often be cleaned and made to work for a while longer. A spray cleaner, of the kind used in radio-television shops, can help, if it is sprayed directly inside the switch.

Replacement switches can be found at appliance dealers. If the switch is a standard on-off switch, it will be easy to find. If it is a special-type switch, you will probably have to get an exact-duplicate replacement from the dealer carrying that line of appliances. Take along the make and model number of the appliance, any part numbers that might be on the switch itself, or, preferably, the old switch. Before disconnecting a switch of the more complicated type with more than two wires, make a sketch of the wires, the switch, and include the wire colors, or put little paper tags on each wire. This will eliminate any chance for mistakes in connecting the new switch.

2

Portable Electric Heaters

Electric heaters are made in many different shapes and sizes but they generally have the same operating features. They are a simple electrical appliance consisting of a heating element, a fan, and a switch. Fig. 2-1 shows the heating element and fan of a typical unit, with one side of the cover removed. This is the "coil-spring" element; others use flat-wire elements wound on a mica card, and some have sealed elements like those on an electric range. Some have thermostats to control the heat, as shown in Fig. 2-2. This thermostat is adjustable and controls both the heating element and the fan motor.

HEATER REPAIRS

There is no doubt about diagnosing the trouble in an electric heater, and it is generally easy to repair. Check the line cord and plug first, as for all other appliances. Many of these use a "heater cord," which is a braid-covered stranded wire wrapped with asbestos, like the type used on electric irons. Others use heavy rubber-coated cord like that used on television sets. Check to see that the wire is not broken inside the insulation near the wall plug; this is the most common trouble. To make sure, take off one side of the cover, plug it in, and check for the presence of a-c voltage at the ends of the line cord; use the little neon tester. If there is voltage at this point but the element will not heat, check through the thermostat. Fig. 2-3 shows how to do this. If there is voltage at the "line" side of the thermostat but none at the load side, the thermostat is not making contact. If there is voltage at the load side of the thermo-

17

stat but the element will not heat, it is definitely open. This is helpful in the case of the "sealed" elements. If your heater has coiled-spring elements, breaks are easy to see. The wire will fall off the supports.

A broken element should be replaced with a new one. If it has been in service long enough to break (caused mostly by corrosion of the heater wire from repeated heating and cooling), the rest of the wire will be brittle and will break again soon. Cleaning off the broken ends and twisting them tightly together will make an emergency repair, but this kind of joint will not last. It will oxidize and break again very shortly. However, this is a good way to keep it going until you can get a replacement element. *Caution:* The exposed-wire type of heating element (like the one shown) is dangerous. Whenever you touch these wires, be sure that the line plug is pulled out and lying where you can see it. You can get a very bad shock from them. If the heater has been turned off for only a moment, you can get a painful burn from touching the wires.

Fig. 2-1. The fan and heating elements of a typical electric heater.

Replacement Elements

You can get replacement elements at any electrical supply store in whatever size you need. Look at the rating-plate of your heater;

Fig. 2-2. Illustrating the thermostat on a typical electric heater.

it will give you the information needed to get an exact duplicate. The coiled elements which you get will be a lot shorter than the original, but they will be the same *electrical* size. To install one of these elements, fasten the two ends, and then very carefully stretch the element over and around the ceramic insulating supports. Do not overdo this, because the element must have enough "spring" left to hold it tightly on the supports. The wires are bare and must *never* be allowed to touch or even come close to the metal of the

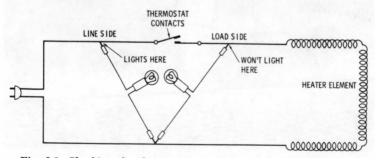

Fig. 2-3. Checking the thermostatic contacts on an electric heater.

case. If the element touches the case, you will have a very dangerous shock hazard.

If you accidentally stretch the element too far, you can sometimes bring it back by pushing the coils back together between your fingers. If it is still slack, tie the element to the ceramic supports with bits of small, bare wire. If you can see a place where the element might touch the case, glue a piece of sheet asbestos to the case under the element. The kind used to cover furnace pipes, etc., will do nicely.

Connections

Many of the older heaters used screw terminals. The newer models use push-on terminals, like those found in your automobile wiring. Fig. 2-4 shows the new element support. Ceramic pins hold the heating element in place, and the element ends have "crimped-on" terminals which connect to resistance wire. You can get these terminals at garages or most radio-parts supply stores. The new element may come with them already mounted, if you get a factory replacement element made by the original manufacturer of your heater. To install one of these crimp-on terminals, scrape the end of the

Fig. 2-4. A typical connector block used on electric heaters.

element wire very clean, push it into the end of the connector, and then crimp it tightly with a pair of small pliers. Crush the sleeve end of the connector until you can be sure that it is making a very good, tight connection. Pull on it, to be sure there is no slack or looseness. To make a tight connection of a small wire in a large connector, double the bare end of the wire to fill up the hole in the end of the connector, then crimp.

On ordinary wires (motor, line cord, etc.) the same type of connectors are used, but these can be soldered if necessary. In fact, you can see a small blob of solder on the motor wire, in Fig. 2-4. If the female connectors are loose on the blade of the male units, very carefully pinch them between the jaws of the pliers, so that they make good tight connections. You should never be able to pull them apart without using a lot of force.

Thermostats

A thermostat is just an automatic switch, operated by heat. Fig. 2-5 shows how the thermostat works. A *bimetal* blade is made so that it bends to the right when it gets too hot and to the left when it gets

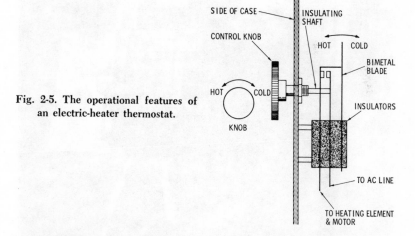

Fig. 2-5. The operational features of an electric-heater thermostat.

cooler. This is done by designing the blade into a sandwich of two different metals, one having a greater coefficient of expansion than the other. The two other blades hold the electrical contacts. An adjustment screw, with a knob on the outside of the case, can be used to set the spacing between the electrical contacts so that they open and close at the desired temperature. The farther the shaft is screwed out (to the left), the longer the contacts will stay closed, until the heat reaches a certain temperature.

To check the thermostat, use the neon tester as mentioned before. Look at the contacts; they may be dark in color, but they should be smooth-surfaced. If they are rough and pitted, they will not make very good contact and should be cleaned. Fig. 2-6 shows a closeup of the thermostat on the heater shown in Fig. 2-1. The contacts in this model are easy to service, but others may have to be loosened and removed to allow cleaning and adjustment. To clean the thermostat contacts, cut a strip of fine sandpaper about ½ inch wide the full length of the sheet. Fold the strip of paper so that the sandy surface is on both sides. Open the contacts and push the sandpaper

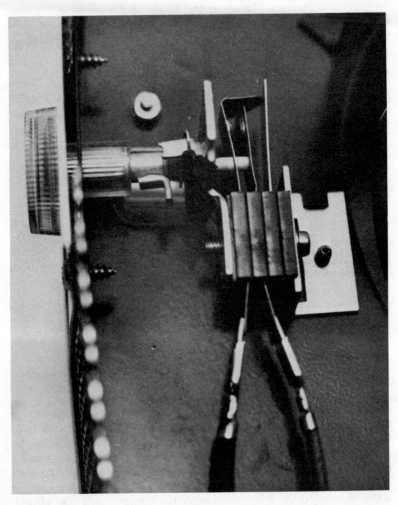

Fig. 2-6. Close-up view of a thermostat control on an electric heater.

through. Hold the contacts together and pull the sandpaper back and forth. Repeat this until the surface of the contacts is smooth and bright. Finish off by cutting a strip from a piece of cardboard, like an old postcard, and pull this through to give the surfaces a high polish. Cardboard is just rough enough to smooth down surfaces like this very nicely.

Check the setting of the thermostat knob to be sure that it will let the contacts close tightly. A loose contact can "chatter," and cause arcing. This will make the contacts burn up again in a short time and you will have your cleaning job to do over. Check all wire terminals to be sure that they are not loose. Loose connections in heavy-current circuits like this will get very hot, burn up, and possibly cause serious trouble.

Switches

Some of these heaters will be equipped with "tip switches." These are safety switches which cut the current off if the heater is accidentally knocked over. A metal rod comes out the bottom of the case and touches the floor. When the heater is sitting in its normal position, the rod is pushed up inside the case and holds a switch closed. If the heater is turned over, a spring pushes the rod down, opening the switch. This is handy, for a radiant heater like this could burn a large hole in a carpet or tile, and can even set a wooden floor on fire if it happened to be turned face down.

Fan Motors

The fan motor can be seen in Fig. 2-2. The motors used in these heaters are small induction-type motors, with solid rotors, and are practically trouble-free. They very seldom need oiling. Turn the fan blade with your fingers; if it spins freely, the fan does not need oil. If the blade "drags," put one drop of oil on each motor

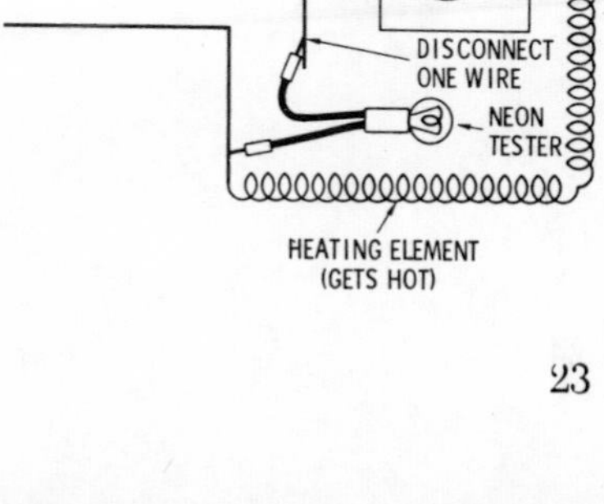

Fig. 2-7. Testing for open motor coil with neon tester.

bearing, and run the motor until it comes back up to normal speed. One drop is enough, for you have only two very small bearings to oil. Too much oil will drip off, and it will usually get onto the heater element, where it will cause a very obnoxious smell.

Turn the heater on, and check with the neon lamp from the open motor wire to the other side of the a-c line as shown in Fig. 2-7. If the lamp glows, the motor coil isn't open. If it doesn't, but the heating element gets hot, then the motor coil is open. If the heater works, this shows that voltage is getting to the unit.

If the lamp glows but the motor will not run, the rotor is probably stuck from lack of oil, frame filled with lint or dust, etc. This is easy to see. Clean out the space inside the motor frame, put in a drop of oil, and spin the rotor with your fingers until it is free. If the fan rattles while running, look for loose bolts in the mounting or loose blades, etc. Some fans are fastened to the motor shaft by setscrews through the hub. If these work loose, then the fan will vibrate and make noises while it is running.

3

Electric Fans

Most houses include an exhaust fan, which is used in the kitchen and/or bathroom to remove unpleasant odors. Another type of fan is the multiple-speed fan used in various rooms to circulate the air for cooling purposes. Various styles can be obtained designed for window or floor use.

EXHAUST FANS

The *exhaust fan* is used in the kitchen, bath, and laundry rooms, etc., and it is a simple fan, mounted in a "through-the-wall" housing. Exhaust fans come in many different shapes and sizes, but they are all basically the same. Motors are standard induction types, without brushes; four-blade fans of fairly high pitch are used, and they are generally "shock-mounted" in rubber bushings to prevent the transfer of noise and shock. Fig. 3-1 shows a typical installation of a wall-mounted exhaust fan. A round or rectangular sheet-metal housing is installed in the wall. A hinged, weatherproof door on the outside, covers the vent opening when the fan is not running. This door can be lifted from the inside, with a chain or lever. A metal arm on the inside of the door operates a push-button switch; when the door is open, the fan is running. When the door is closed, the arm pushes on the switch, stopping the fan motor.

An ornamental grille covers the inner opening. The grille is usually chromed, but can be any color, painted to match the decor. It is usually held in place by a long screw which fits a threaded stud on the end of the motor itself. The fan motor is mounted on three or

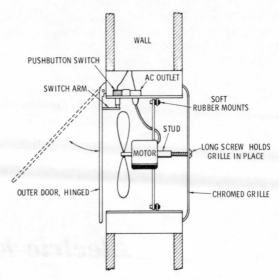

Fig. 3-1. A wall-mounted exhaust fan.

four metal arms. These are fitted with soft rubber bushings, to reduce noise. A typical fan and grille unit is shown in Fig. 3-2. The three supporting arms are on top, and the long grille-mounting stud can be seen as well. Note the short line cord used. This is plugged into a special single outlet which is mounted on the inside of the house, as is the control switch.

Most fan motors of this type are permanently lubricated, with good-sized oil wicks in each end bell. If the fan seems to be running

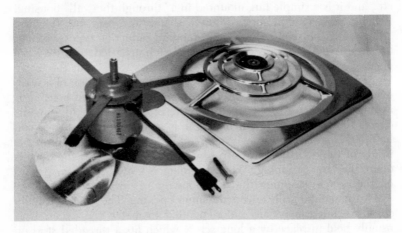

Fig. 3-2. Illustrating an exhaust-fan motor and grille.

too slowly, turn it off, take off the grille, and spin the blades with your fingers. If the fan has enough oil, the blades should coast for a long time after a flip with a finger. If they seem to drag, the fan may need oiling. Most units of this type will have to be removed for oiling; however, some may have oil holes that are accessible without the fan being dismounted and some can be oiled from outside the house. Fill the oil holes with a light oil; this will take only a few

Fig. 3-3. Disassembling exhaust-fan motor.

drops. Spin the blades, or start the motor for a few seconds. After this oil has soaked into the felt wicks, add a few more drops. Wipe off any excess oil; it would catch dust.

If the motor still binds, remove the motor from the fan housing, and tear it down. Take the blades off first; these are usually held on the shaft by a setscrew. Take the mounting brackets off by removing the nuts with a nutdriver or small wrench, as shown in Fig. 3-3. There will be two more nuts under the mounting arms which hold the motor housing together. Take these off, and carefully pry the two halves of the motor apart with a small screwdriver. Check the felt wicks for oil and see if the motor windings show signs of overheating or if the motor itself is clogged with lint. Most motors used in this kind of service are "sealed" almost airtight to keep out dirt and lint, but the finer particles will, in time, fill the motor.

Check the condition of the shafts at the bearings; these will be close to the rotor itself. The shafts should have a mirrorlike polish. If the shaft is dirty, dull or scored, it must be smoothed off and new bearings installed; the old bearings are definitely worn out. Another symptom of bearing failure is a loud buzzing or rattling noise when the fan is running. After taking the blades off, run the motor. The rattle may have been due to a loose rivet, etc., on the blades, instead of a bad motor. A motor without the blades should make very little noise when running. If the motor does not start when the outer door is lifted, check the line cord, the outlet, and the switch. Be sure that the arm hits the switch when the door is closed. Pull the plug, open the door, and check the outlet to make sure that there is actually a-c voltage present. If voltage is present at the outlet, but the fan will not run, then either the motor may be bad or the line cord broken.

You can check the fan motor for operation by holding the fan blades with your left hand, and applying voltage to the motor. The fan will hum and try to run, but these motors have a very low starting torque, and they can easily be held by the fingertips. In fact, it will not hurt the motor to hold it still for up to one or two minutes. This applies *only* to the smaller type of fan. Do not try this with the bigger-type motors with ¼ hp or more. The push-button switch and outlet will be mounted on the inside of the housing with a couple of small screws. Connections will be made from the house wiring with pigtails, or to terminal screws on the body of the switch and outlet. Before taking the switch unit out, be *sure* that the power is turned off at the load center. When the fan is first installed, find out which circuit breaker supplies the voltage.

This can be accomplished by turning the fan on, and then flipping one circuit breaker after another until you find the one that turns off the fan. Write the number of this breaker on the inside of the fan housing with a soft-lead pencil for future information. If the switch is defective, it can be replaced; take the old one along with you to be sure of getting the right size. If necessary, the whole switch/outlet unit can be replaced without too much expense. When you put the switch/outlet unit back, be very sure that all your connections are tight and well-insulated. If terminal screws are used, make sure that the wire insulation goes right up to the screw head. If wirenuts and pigtails are used, be sure that there is no bare wire exposed after the wirenuts are tightened. If there is any doubt, cover each joint with at least two wraps of vinyl plastic electrician's tape. Bare wires can be a very definite fire hazard, since the connection is inside the wall; do not take *any* chances. This connection should be made in an "outlet box," but, even so, you do not want to have any short circuits.

Cooking gives off fairly large quantities of grease-laden smoke. If an exhaust fan is mounted directly over a cooking stove, it will pump this air outdoors as soon as possible; this is what it is designed to do. However, it will also intercept a good deal of the grease. This is unavoidable and it often is necessary to give the unit a good cleaning. This is especially true if these is a screen on the unit. The screen will pick up a coating of grease, and this will cause lint and dust to accumulate. In time, the screen may be completely clogged from this accumulation. To clean the screen, remove it from the fan unit and wash the grease off with a solvent. You can use the kind of solvent used by dry cleaners or even, in emergencies, kerosense. *Do not* use gasoline or any other inflammable solvent. A less dangerous way is to make up about a quart of solution, using water and a cupful of detergent. Immerse the screen in the solution and let it soak for about 5 minutes. Then scrub it vigorously with an old paintbrush or toothbrush. Soak it again and then flush off the residue under a faucet or with a hose. Dry it thoroughly before putting it back.

The motor, mountings, and fan blades will often pick up heavy accumulations of this dust. In bad cases, the fan blades can even become unbalanced by dirt accumulated on one or more blades. Use the same cleaning solution on the blades, but be careful not to bend the blades; this could cause noise. If the switch and outlet are on the bottom of the housing, be careful not to "slop" too much around this section. Turn off the a-c power before the cleanup job. If the switch is on the top, water will not damage the electrical parts, but it is still a good idea to turn the power off before doing any work inside the housing.

MULTIPLE-SPEED FANS

Electric fans come in many different types, and one of the most popular is the multiple-speed type. This is not the old original multi-speed "oscillating fan" in a round cage, but comes in a rectangular case or cabinet. It can be set on the floor or in the window sill, and the speed selector allows the user to get the amount of air he wants or needs. A stamped-steel case, with grilles on both sides as guards, is used on most units. They come in all sizes from 8 to 20 inches in diameter—big enough to cool a good-sized room or meeting hall. There are even bigger models, usually having heavy motors and mounted on floor stands. Some of the home types have adjustable steel-rod stands so that the fan itself can be set to blow at any desired angle, up or down.

Fig. 3-4 shows a typical home unit, a 20-inch fan with three speeds. One grille has been removed and the selector switch taken

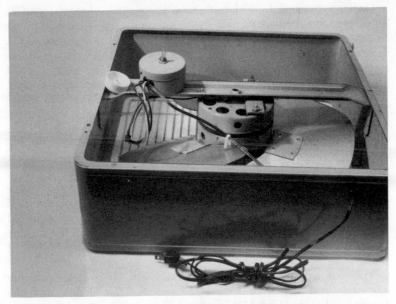

Fig. 3-4. A typical multiple-speed electric fan.

off to show its construction. The switch is enclosed in a sheet-metal container to keep dirt and dust from accumulating on the switch. These fans use specially wound motors. In the older types, an external resistance device added in series with the motor was used to slow it down. This wasted power and generated *heat*. This kind of control was "self-defeating," because the fan was supposed to cool the place, not add more heat. By means of the speed-selector switch shown in Fig. 3-5 three different field-windings can be switched in. By making each winding with the right characteristics, any desired speed can be obtained. This motor uses a laminated rotor with no windings and no brushes. The rotor itself is the only moving part, and all the attention this type of motor needs is an occasional drop of light oil on the bearings about once a month, if the fan is used quite often.

Oil holes, with a tube leading to the oil wick in the bearing, can be reached by removing the grille. The fan must be in an upright position, so that the oil will run down the tube into the wick (Fig. 3-6). The speed-selector switch is held on by a thin ½-inch hex nut, which also holds the escutcheon plate. A small adjustable wrench will get this nut off easily. A ⅜-inch nutdriver will remove the grille screws. The wrench will do it, though not so quickly.

The most likely source of trouble in this kind of fan will be the speed-selector switch itself. With practically no moving parts, the motors give very little trouble. A dirty switch contact can cause one or more speeds to go dead. If a fan will run on any one speed, the chances are that the motor is in good operating condition. For example, if it will run on "medium," but not on "fast" or "slow," the switch is almost sure to be defective. Fig. 3-7 shows a close-up view

Fig. 3-5. Three-speed selector switch used in multiple-speed electric fans.

of a typical switch, resting on the protective case. Note the "push-on" terminals. You can check this type of switch with your neon test-lamp, if it seems to be giving trouble. There will be one wire, from the a-c cord, that does not connect to the switch. This is the "common," and it is usually connected to the white wire going to the motor. The "hot" side of the a-c line cord goes to the common terminals of the switch.

If one speed or more refuses to work, remove the line plug and position switch as shown in Fig. 3-7. Mark the color of each wire on the body of the switch at the proper terminal. If you cannot write on the switch, make up a rough pencil sketch of how the wires are connected, so that you will know how to put them back. Turn the switch to the "off," position for a reference point, then count "clicks" to be sure just which position you are in. For example, if the "medium" will not work, you need two clicks from "off." Now, take the "fast" or "slow" wire, and touch this to the "medium" switch terminal. Now, plug the line cord back into the socket, and if the motor runs, then the "medium" field-winding is defective. If it does not operate, then there is a defective contact on "medium" position in the switch. For a cross-check, put the "medium" wire on either the "fast" or "slow" terminals. If the motor runs, this is definite proof that the switch is bad. Replacement switches can be found at the

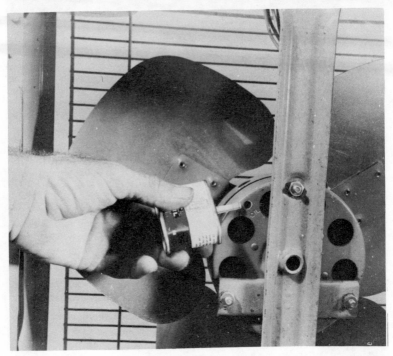

Fig. 3-6. Oiling a fan motor.

appliance dealers, and an exact duplicate is always best; take along the old one as a sample.

You can check for voltage at any of the switch terminals with the neon tester. With all power *off*, push the thin tip of the test-prod up inside the wirenut holding the common wires. Then check for glow on each of the switch terminals, beginning with the other side of the a-c line. By moving the switch to each position and checking for voltage at the motor wire, you can tell whether it is making the proper contact. If the switch seems to be intermittent, i.e., runs one time but refuses to run the next time it is turned on, the switch could very well be dirty. This is normally the result due to wear and old age, and the best way to cure it is with a brand new switch. In a

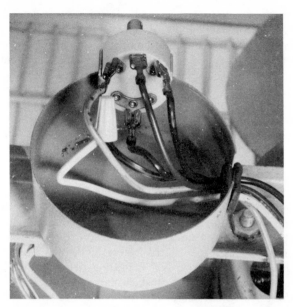

Fig. 3-7. Illustrating a three-speed selector switch.

very few cases, it can be cleaned by spraying cleaning compound inside the case but this is usually only a temporary measure.

If you suspect that the switch is bad (not making contact at all), although the neon tester shows that there is a-c on the line cord terminals, take a piece of well-insulated wire to use as a jumper. With the power on, touch one end of this wire to the a-c line terminal of the switch, and the other to one of the motor wires. If the motor starts, the switch is definitely bad. As soon as the motor starts to run, yank the jumper wire off. That's all you wanted to know and you don't want that fan running full-speed without any guards. *Be very careful when making this kind of test.* You are handling "hot" wires and there are a lot of loose wires lying about. Handle wires *only* by the insulation. Never touch any of the bare terminals unless you can see the line plug of this appliance lying on the bench in plain sight. Incidentally, make *sure* that the plug you see is the one that goes with *this* appliance and not from some other equipment. As the writer can testify, this is an easy mistake to make and the results can be very painful.

Let us assume that the worst has happened: the nut that holds the switch has loosened and the switch has been twisted around until all wires have been pulled off. Now, the problem is: "Which one goes where?" Let's start with the easiest one—the line cord. Check to make sure that the common is still fastened tightly to the common motor wire, and that no bare wire is showing. Next, find the other side of the line cord, which is easy. On the switch, this will go to an easily identifiable terminal; note the three rivets in the switch in the photo. If the switch is still in good operating condition, connect the wire to proper connector. If the connectors have been pulled off (a very common trouble), strip about ¼ inch of insulation from each wire, straighten the strands, and lay the bar end in the little groove in the end of the push-on connector and solder the connection. If you have new connectors and the proper crimping-tool, you can use these, but in an emergency, solder them as described. Make sure that the solder joint is firm, and that the insulation is as close to the joint as possible. Put the connectors back on all the wires.

Now, plug the three wires into the switch in any order, and try it. The escutcheon plate will tell you in which order they should work. In this one, it happens to be "off," "fast," "medium," and, finally, "slow." Start with No. 1, and run through all three positions. See which one sounds as if it were the fastest. Say this is No. 3. Pull the wire off No. 3 and put it on No. 1, putting No. 1 on No. 3. Try it again. Now you should have "fast" where it belongs, and all you need to do is see which one of the remaining two is the faster; this will be "medium," and once you get it in the right place, the other one is pretty simple; there is only one terminal left. *Now* mark the wire colors for each speed on the switch or on the inside of the fan housing, so that you will not have this same trouble the next time. Put the switch back in position and tighten the nut. Use a lock-washer to keep it tight. Replace the knob, which is almost always just a "push-on" type, and the job is done.

You can use the same method on the switches which have the wires soldered in place. Use the same precautions about pulling the line plug before working with any wiring. Locate and hook up the a-c line cord to the common, if it needs it. Now strip the ends of each wire as before, and solder the strands together. There will still be plenty of solder left on the switch terminals. Now "tack" each wire to a terminal, a-c line-cord wire first as before, and test it. To make a "tack-joint," simply hold the tinned end of a wire on the terminal and touch it with the tip of a soldering iron until the solder melts; hold it in place until the solder sets. After you have located "fast" or any one speed, you can make a proper solder joint as before. Clean the old solder out of the hole in the terminal, and pass the end of the wire through it, and then resolder it neatly. Check out the other two speeds as before, solder leads in place, and the job is done.

There are many different types of fans; some have only two speeds, others have three, and others are even *reversible*, with three speeds in each direction. This allows the user to set it in a window, for example, and blow out hot air during the day and pull in cool air during the night. All of them work in exactly the same way as the one described, with simpler or more complicated selector switches. The same tests and service methods will work on any of them. If a fan develops a rattling noise while running, look for something loose. Even a loose guard-grille screw can cause a very annoying vibration and rattle. If the hub gets loose on the motor shaft or one of the blades is loose, this will also raise quite a fuss. The hub is usually fastened to the shaft with a setscrew. A great many fans use *Allen* screws; these have a hollow hex-shaped hole instead of a slot or cross, and they require a special wrench. This is a simple hexagonal-shaped *L* rod which can be found, in sets of several sizes, at all auto supply and radio-television supply stores.

Fig. 3-8 illustrates an *Allen* wrench being used to take off the hub and blade assembly. The hub assembly here is steel, and the aluminum blades are riveted to the arms. If the hub is still tight on the shaft, check the blades for loose rivets. One of these can cause a terriffc rattling. To retighten a loose rivet, take the hub and blade assembly off, and hold the rivet over a very solid backup block, a vise, or a good-sized piece of flat steel, and tap the other end of the rivet lightly with a ball-peen hammer. Do not hit hard; you will get

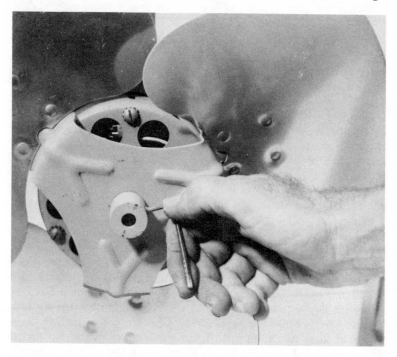

Fig. 3-8. Removing blade and hub assembly using an *Allen* wrench.

much better results by tapping lightly until the rivet expands and fills up the hole again. One hard blow will often bend the shank of the rivet and distort the hole, which will make it very hard to ever get a new rivet tight again.

While working on the blades, be very careful not to bend them out of position. Two blades in line and two bent out will unbalance the fan, especially at high speeds. Of course, changing the angle of attack of any one blade will do the same thing; the bent blade has a different air-resistance than the others, and this causes an aerodynamic unbalance. Translated, this means that the fan will vibrate like crazy when running fast, and probably walk off the table. If a blade has been accidentally bent, remove the unit, and lay it on a table or bench with a perfectly *flat* surface, hub side up. If only one

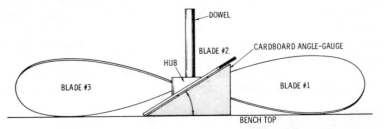

Fig. 3-9. A test template used for checking blade angles.

blade of a four-blade fan (which most of them are) is bent, you will be able to see which one is out of line and make that one line up with the rest. The tips of all blades should touch the table.

Check the blade angles by making a template out of cardboard cut in the shape of a triangle at the proper angle, which will be about 15 degrees in most fans. By shoving this triangular gauge under each blade, you can tell whether it is set properly. Fig. 3-9 shows how this is done. Set all blades to the *same* angle. A few degrees off will not matter if the fan is otherwise in good shape, but one blade at one angle, and the rest at another, definitely will cause a vibration.

Fig. 3-10 shows an alignment jig which you can make for your bench. This will be a great help in checking blade angles. Get a small rod of about the same size as the motor shaft; a wooden dowel will do. Fit this into the top of your bench so that it is exactly perpendicular to the bench top. You can do this by drilling a hole just a tiny bit larger than the rod, and then correcting by driving little wooden wedges into the proper side. Check it for vertical by measuring at least two sides with a carpenter's try square. No matter where you put the square, it should show that the rod sits at exactly a right angle to the bench top.

36

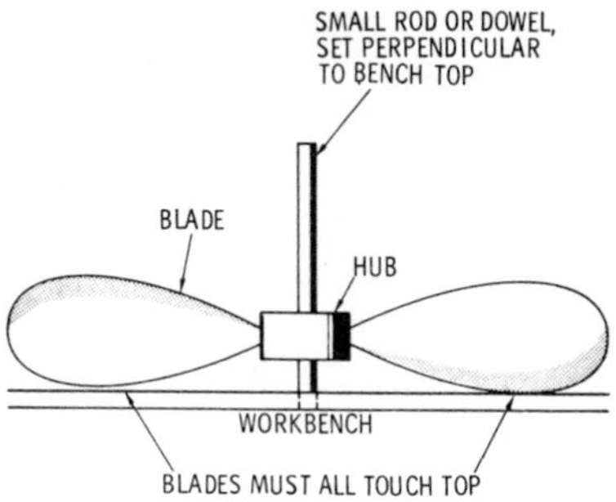

Fig. 3-10. An alignment jig made to
check balance of blade.

BLADE

HUB

WORKBENCH

BLADES MUST ALL TOUCH TOP

You can check the "fore and after" positions of the blade tips. The
tip of each blade should touch the bench top at the same point on
the blade itself. This must also be used for angle checking. The use
of this will help to get rid of the very common error made in setting
blades by a calibrated eyeball. This makes the fan blade wobble a
great deal and causes a terrific vibration. For a quick check of blade
alignment before you take the fan apart, watch the blades from the
side. Turn the fan off and watch the blades as they coast to a stop.
When they are almost stopped, any wobble or misalignment will be
much more apparent; at high speeds the blades are moving too fast
for you to notice any variation.

4

Electric Knives and Toothbrushes

Electric knives and toothbrushes are fast becoming a very popular household item. Electric knives can reduce carving time by one half giving the housewife more free time. The electric toothbrush cleans teeth much better, especially for children, and also reduces brushing time.

ELECTRIC KNIVES

The electric carving knife comes in two types: standard and cordless. Unlike most cordless devices, these can be repaired; the rest are permanently sealed units. Most electric knives are basically the same. A small electric motor drives a worm gear and pinion. This converts the rotary motion of the motor to a reciprocating motion, so that the two blades go back and forth very rapidly to give the slicing action. Fig. 4-1 shows how this worm-and-pinion drive works.

ELECTRIC MODELS

In the cord models, a small brush-type a-c motor drives the blades. The motor in the cordless type looks similar to the a-c motor, but operates from direct current. The power comes from a set of nickel-cadmium rechargeable batteries in the handle. A charging unit in the stand keeps a small "trickle charge" on the batteries whenever the knife is set in the stand, so that it is ready for instant use. A fully

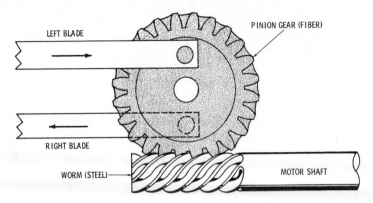

Fig. 4-1. Worm-and-pinion drive for an electric carving knife.

charged set of batteries will run the motor for quite some time. Repairs to either type of knife will involve about the same amount of labor since the two are almost identical. So, we will discuss the motor and associated parts first and cover the batteries and charger later.

The cases are made of plastic, in two sections. They are held together by small screws, usually *Phillips*-head types. Some have small lugs on the front end which slip into slots on the bottom half of the case, and one or two screws holding the back. Make sure that you have all of the screws out before trying to pry the case apart. Never use force, or you will break the case. When all fastenings are loose, the case will come apart very easily. With the detachable half of the case off, the unit will look like the illustration in Fig. 4-2. It can

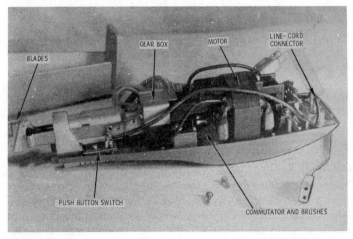

Fig. 4-2. The mechanical parts of a typical electric knife.

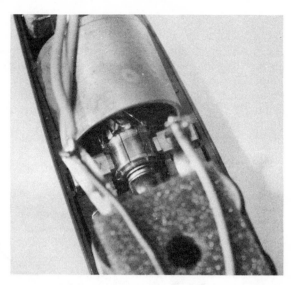

Fig. 4-3. The commutator and brushes of a cordless
electric knife.

be operated for testing in this condition. If the motor is laboring, the
knife blades running slow, check the worm gear and pinion for
lubrication. See that moving parts are not tight or binding. These
parts should be packed with a creamy lubricant so that it will not
drip out on the food.

Check the motor brushes and the commutator (see Fig. 4-3). The
surface of the commutator should be smooth. It may be darkened,
but, as long as it is smooth, the commutator should operate. The
brushes can usually be checked by eye for wear, since the brush
holders have slots in them. If the brushes have worn off too much,
they will lose tension, jump, and arc. This will cause the commutator
to pit and burn. If the brushes are replaced, clean up the commutator to make the new ones last longer. Install the new brushes and
start the motor. Cut a piece of very fine sandpaper about ¼ inch
wide and 8 to 10 inches long. Do not use emery cloth, because it
leaves a conducting residue which can get between the commutator
bars and cause a short. Fold the sandpaper over the end of a thin
wooden stick or a nail board, to keep away from the brushes and
terminals, which can bite. Hold the end of the sandpaper flat on the
commutator. When the sandpaper wears down, fold it to expose a
fresh piece. Keep this up until the commutator surface is clean and
smooth.

New brushes can be purchased from the dealer handling this
make of appliance or from any electric appliance repair shop. Make

sure that you get the correct brush, so that it will slide freely in the holder and not stick. In most of these motors, the brush holders can be removed easily by taking out a couple of small screws. This frees a thin metal spring-plate which holds the brush holders down under a couple of thin phenolic insulators. Check the fine-braided copper wire which feeds current to the brushes. If too many of the strands are broken, the wire will not carry enough current, and the motor will not come up to speed, and it will overheat. When replacing the wire, be sure that these wires are dressed so that they will not short to any other metal parts.

The motors seldom need oiling; most of them are fitted with oilless bearings, made of a sintered (fine-powder) metal. This metal has millions of tiny pores which hold oil, releasing it if the bearing gets hot. If the motor seems to need oil, put one drop (no more) of very fine oil on each bearing. If you hear the motor speed up, then it did need lubrication. *Do not over-oil.* One drop is enough to oil a bearing like this for at least a year of service. If the motor will not run at all, check the line cord. Look for broken wires near the plug or plugs. In cord models, a female plug like the interlock used on a television set is used on the knife end. Most cord troubles happen close to the ends, for this is where the maximum bending takes place. Snap a rubber band around the switch, to hold it on, and then work the cord back and forth, pulling and pushing. If you hear the motor start suddenly, you have a broken line cord.

If the break is near the wall-plug end, you can cut off about 6 inches of the cord and put on a new plug. The little interlock plug on the other end is molded to the cord, and is not replaceable; a new cord must be purchased. You can also check the cord with one of the little neon voltage-testers. Apply voltage, and touch the test probes to the line terminals in the knife housing. If the neon lamp does not glow, the cord is broken. The same trouble can be caused by a bad on-off switch. If there is voltage at the end of the cord but the motor will not run when the switch is pushed, put the rubber band around it to hold it closed, and check across the switch terminals with the neon lamp as shown in Fig. 4-4. If the lamp glows, the switch is not making contact. The switch terminals are a handy place to make voltage tests. One side goes to the a-c line, and the other to the motor. If the neon lamp glows with the switch open, then the line cord and motor have voltage, at least, they do have continuity up to this point.

Push the button and look at the switch contacts to see if they are moving. Normally, the top (movable) blade should push down, touching the bottom blade and making contact. The switch contacts close and then wipe across each other each time the switch is closed. This wiping action helps to keep the contacts clean. If the bottom

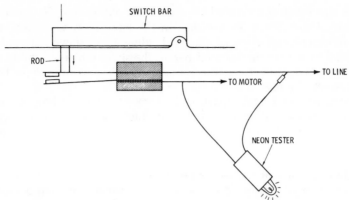

Fig. 4-4. Checking the on-off switch on an electric knife.

blade is bent down too far, the contacts will not touch. Carefully bend the bottom blade up until the contacts touch, making the bottom blade bend a little when the button is pushed all the way down. Whenever you make any adjustments to the switch, brushes, etc., make sure that the line cord is pulled out of the wall outlet and lying on the bench where you can *see* the plug.

If the contacts are dirty, use a piece of very fine sandpaper or crocus cloth, and cut a strip about ¼ inch wide. Slip this between the contacts, hold the button down, and pull it through. Turn it over, and do this again to clean the other side. Keep it up until you can see that the surface of the contacts is smooth and shiny. Then adjust the blades so that the contacts close firmly. If you want to put a really good shine on the contacts, cut a strip of heavy cardboard, perhaps a postal card, and pull this through between the contacts. This puts a high gloss on the contact surface and makes the switch last longer. If the motor operates, but the blades will not move, then the trouble is in the worm gear and pinion. Since the worm is cut into the end of the motor shaft itself, and is made of very hard steel, it very seldom gives trouble. The pinion gear is deliberately made of a phenolic plastic, so that it will take any wear and also make the system run more quietly. The most common trouble in cases like this is that the teeth are worn off of the pinion. If this is true, it will have to be replaced.

Take off the pinion gear clamp or housing. Most of these are some kind of bracket, held down by four small screws (Fig. 4-5). Remove the bracket, and the pinion gear and shaft will lift up and out. You can purchase a new gear assembly from the dealer for this make of appliance. The sliders which drive the blade will have holes in the inner ends. These fit over small studs or dogs on each side of the pinion. If the pinion is turning but the slider or sliders are not moving, these dogs are sheared off; the pinion will have to be replaced. Some of the sliders fit into slots in the knife housing; others may have sheet-metal clips or clamps holding them down. These will probably have to be taken off before the slider-pinion assembly can be lifted out. Do not use force; when all of the fastenings have been taken off, the unit will come apart very easily.

When you take this apart, make a rough sketch of how it looks, where each part goes, etc., because it might be some time until you start putting it back together. This will make the reassembly a whole lot easier. The thin metal blade-latches, locks, etc. fit into slots and grooves in the nylon sliders, and every part must be in exactly the right place or you will never get it to work again. After taking the sliders and latches out, slip them back together and snap a rubber band around the assembled unit; this will keep it "in order" until you get ready to reassemble it. You probably will not need any extra lubricant, but if a new part is installed, put a small amount of cream lubricant on the unit. This special lubricant is sold in radio and appliance stores under the name of *Lubriplate* and other trade names. It is a fairly viscous white lubricant, and it will stick to the gears, etc. and not drop out. Do not use any kind of oil on these parts. Some silicone grease, although it is very expensive, will do a good job of lubrication.

Fig. 4-5. Worm-and-pinion assembly.

CORDLESS MODELS

The battery-operated cordless types have a battery unit made up of five nickel-cadmium cells, as shown in Fig. 4-6. Notice that the

44

batteries are connected with welded straps. This eliminates the possibility that the intercell connections will corrode or get dirty. If your unit uses flashlight cells, make sure that all connections, springs, etc., are clean and bright, and that the clamps hold the cells very tightly for best electrical contact. The individual cells look like common flashlight batteries, but are rechargeable. In the one shown, a five-cell unit gives a voltage of 6.0 volts dc, or 1.2 volts per cell. Fully charged, the open-circuit voltage of the five-cell group will measure about 7 volts on a d-c voltmeter. This can be checked without taking the housing apart, by measuring the charging terminals on the back

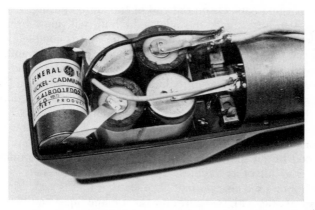

Fig. 4-6. Battery unit for cordless carving knives.

of the housing; the batteries are connected directly across this point. To get an accurate reading, hook up the voltmeter, and push the on-off button—take the voltage reading under full load, with the motor running. The voltage should stay up to about 5.7 volts. If it drops to about 4.0 volts, the battery needs recharging.

If the voltage drops below 4.0 volts when the motor is running, and will not come up after an overnight charge, then one of the cells may be dead. It could also be caused by a dirty on-off switch; check this first, since it is easier. Take the case apart, push the switch button, and measure the voltage across each cell of the battery in turn. This should be at least 1.1 volt for the individual cells. If any cell shows about half this voltage or even reverses in polarity when the motor is running, it would indicate a dead cell. The whole battery unit will have to be replaced. In fact, even if this uses separate-cell batteries, it is not a good idea to replace only one cell if the batteries have been used for more than 2 or 3 months. All new fresh cells should be installed.

The battery unit is soldered in place, which keeps the connections from developing a high-resistance joint. Long metal arms are connected to the batteries, and wires from the motor and switch are soldered to the arms. When you take these off, be sure to make a sketch of the connections showing the wire colors, so that you get them back with the right polarity. The motor will run either way, but if you hook the batteries up backward, they will not recharge. The positive wire is usually *red* and the negative *black*, but this is not always observed. You do not have to have an expensive voltmeter to test batteries or charging unit. Obtain a pilot light and socket of the type used on radio and television sets. Solder a couple of short wires to the terminals. To check the battery, touch the wires to the charging contacts on the end of the knife housing. If the batteries are fully charged, the pilot-light bulb will glow brightly. A dim glow or no light at all means that the unit is completely dead.

You can use the same equipment to check the charger unit. There is no switch on most of the charger units, since it draws no current unless the knife is sitting in its holder. Touch the wires to the contacts on the bottom of the well where the knife sits. If the pilot light glows brightly, the charger is operating. This light takes 6.3 volts at 150 milliamperes, which is about the normal load for this type of charger unit. If it will deliver enough current to light the pilot light to a good bright glow, it is in good shape. The charger units used in this and all other cordless appliances are *solid-state modules*. Fig. 4-7 shows the charger unit. The charger unit is sealed in a solid block of plastic, with two wires for the a-c line input and two for the battery terminals. Incidentally, this unit will not run the motor by itself; the batteries must be in place. It is intended only to put a very small trickle charge into the batteries to keep them up to normal charge.

Fig. 4-8 illustrates a typical charger-unit power supply. The a-c line connects to a capacitor in series which drops the voltage for charging the batteries. The silicon rectifier converts the alternating current into the required direct current. Incidentally, the term *solid-state* refers to the silicon rectifier, and not to the fact that the unit is sealed in a solid block. If you have a d-c volt-ammeter, you can measure the output voltage and current. This unit, with a 6.0-volt battery, has a maximum output of 9 volts across a completely charged battery, at a current of 150 milliamperes. This is why we can check the output accurately with a 150-ma pilot-light bulb. This voltage output depends on the total number and type of batteries used in your unit. Five flashlight batteries would have a voltage of 7.5 volts, at 1.5 volts per cell.

If the charger has no output, do not replace the unit until you have checked the line cord, which goes into one side and is sealed

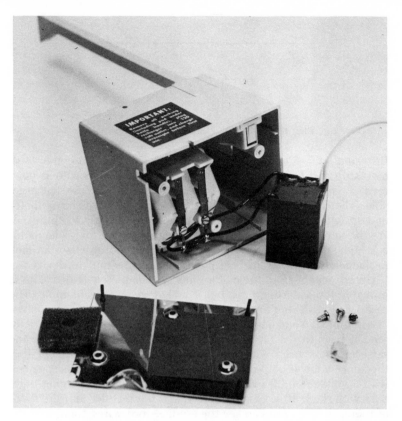

Fig. 4-7. Interior view of a charger unit.

in place. It could be broken at the other end, near the wall plug. For a conclusive test, carefully pull the two wires apart, and scrape a place on the insulation until you can see the bare wires. Now, apply voltage and touch the tips of the neon tester test leads to the bare wires. Keep your fingers clear. If the neon bulb does not glow, the cord is open. Get a new cord, and clip the wires where you stripped the insulation for this test. Splice and tape this well, and tuck the splice inside the charger-unit housing for protection and neater appearance. If there is a-c voltage at this point where the line goes into the module, but no d-c output voltage, the module unit will have to be replaced.

ELECTRIC TOOTHBRUSHES

The electric toothbrush is a simple device. A tiny battery-powered motor drives a *wobbler* gear-device, which makes the brush oscillate.

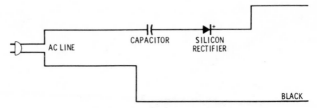

Fig. 4-8. A typical charger-unit power supply.

Instead of a back and forth motion as in the electric knife, the brush moves *up* and *down* to give the correct brushing action. It is powered by self-contained nickel-cadmium cells which are rechargeable. The charging unit is in the stand or base in which the motor unit sits when not in use. Motors used in most electric toothbrushes are the same type as those used in battery-powered toys. The motor is a high-speed d-c motor about an inch long and less than an inch in diameter, with an amazing power for such a minute device.

Unfortunately all of the motor units are completely sealed. This is probably for watertightness, but it makes them nonrepairable. The cases are plastic and are cemented together so that they can not be disassembled. Your only recourse if the motor unit goes bad is to send it back to the factory for repairs. The charging units are the same as those used with the cordless electric knives, except that they have a lower output voltage. Most of these seem to use one cell with a voltage of 1.2 volts. Fig. 4-9 shows a typical charging unit/base with the bottom cover removed and the rectifier unit lifted out of the enclosure. You can see the a-c line-cord wires going into the

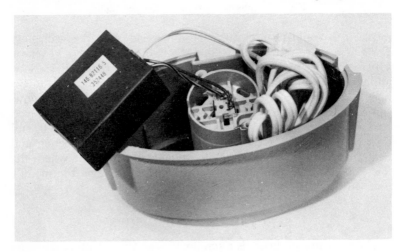

Fig. 4-9. Charger unit for an electric toothbrush.

box and the battery wires coming out to the charging terminals, in the center. The only thing you can do is replace the charging unit with a new one, if it fails.

You can test these units in the same manner as for the cordless knives, by using a small penlight bulb. One of these bulbs should have a dim light since the voltage will be a little less than 1.2 volts. If it lights at all, the charger unit is working. Symptoms of charger trouble would be the failure of the unit to take a charge; it will run for a few seconds and then stop, or not run at all if the battery is completely discharged. Before blaming the charging unit, make sure that the socket in the base is making good contact when the toothbrush is set back for storage. Normally, you should feel just a little bit of resistance when you push it back into the base.

Looking down into the base with the toothbrush removed you will be able to see the two terminals. One will be in the center and the other on the outside. Most of the bases are built somewhat like a socket, although a few have "spring" contacts. In the socket types, bend the little blades closer together so that they grip the pin firmly. On the spring or plate contacts, smooth and brighten them with fine sandpaper so that all corrosion is removed. With the motor working on such low voltage and such small currents, it takes only a very little bit of resistance in a dirty contact to stop the unit from charging. If there are no exposed wires in the line cord going into the charging unit, carefully nip off just a little insulation on each wire, at points about an inch apart. This exposes the wires of the line cord, and you can check with the neon tester to see if there is a-c power getting to the charger. If there is a-c power but no charger output, the charger block is definitely bad.

You can get replacement chargers at any dealer who handles this make. It is a good idea to leave all wires hooked up until you get the replacement unit. If you cannot, then clip the wires off instead of unsoldering them, leaving about an inch of wire on each terminal. This is an old television technician's trick, and it saves a lot of time in hooking up new replacement parts. A rough sketch of the unit and connections, showing wire colors and locations, can be made so that you will not get the wires reversed. The line cord will probably be a part of the new unit, so all you will have to worry with will be the battery wires.

5

Electric Hair Driers

Wherever there is a woman, the chances are that there is a hair drier stowed away somewhere. With today's elaborate hair-dos, they are a necessity, not a luxury. Any trouble with the hair drier usually results in an emergency, and the home handyman can build up a lot of goodwill by being able to fix it when it quits at the wrong time. Although there is a tremendous difference in outward appearance, size, etc., hair driers are generally alike on the inside. They include a fan which blows air through a soft plastic hose to a thin plastic bonnet. The bonnet is slipped over the head and tied with a drawstring. It is generally in two layers, with vent holes inside, so that the hot air is distributed evenly over the hair-do. An electric heater in the fan housing warms the air to speed the drying. Basically that is all there is to a hair drier—a fan, heater, and bonnet.

All but the very simplest have a selector switch so that the heater can be switched on and off, to give cool, warm, or hot air circulation. Some have push buttons, others have rotary switches, and some use separate slide switches. In some designs, the fan switch also controls the heater, so that the fan must be running before the heater can be turned on. We will cover as many different makes and models as possible, but if your particular unit is not covered, remember that all are similar in operation, and you can use the same test and repair methods in most cases.

DIAGNOSIS OF TROUBLE

In most units there are two basic parts: the motor and fan and the heater. For the first test, we must find out if it is the motor or the heater, or both. If the drier will not operate, the troubles could be in the line cord or switch. Check for a-c voltage at the inner end of the cord, and then by-pass the switch. If the fan does not run because the motor is stuck, etc., but the heater is getting hot, turn it off immediately. A lot of housings are made in soft thermoplastic material, and they can be damaged by too much heat.

Disassembly

To disassemble the unit, first look for screws which hold the case together. The cases are usually made in two sections, with the motor, fan, and heater mounted on one part. Fig. 5-1 shows a typical unit, taken apart to show the construction. You can see the fan motor, heaters, control switches, and the air duct mounted on the main

Fig. 5-1. A typical hair-drier disassembled to show various parts.

frame. *Phillips* screws seem to be the favorite fasteners. These are screwed into the ends of plastic studs molded into the case. Be sure that you get all of them out before trying to pull the two halves apart. If it does not come apart easily, you have missed a screw somewhere, and do not use force. Check it over carefully, and you will find the missing screw. Lift up carefully on one side of the case, and you will be able to tell which side is still fastened.

If you are unlucky and break a stud or if the machine has been dropped, cracking the case, it can be repaired with epoxy resin cement, which is sold at all auto supply and radio stores. You can often find out which type of plastic is used in the case and get just the right cement at a radio supply house. To find out, put a drop of the cement on the inside of the case. If this can be wiped off without leaving a mark, in about 10 seconds, it is not the right cement. The right cement will dissolve a little bit of the plastic and leave a rough surface. The thermoplastic cases can be repaired with a hot soldering iron or hot spatula. Hold the cracked place tightly together, and run the tip of the iron along the crack, on the inside of the case. This type of plastic will soften. Then run the edges back together so that they will harden again when cool. One of the flame thrower or pipe-lighter types of cigarette lighter is a handy tool for use in repairing cases.

On other plastics with bad breaks, cut a strip of thin cloth and spread plastic cement the length of the crack and about an inch wide. Lay the cloth over the crack, and press it down firmly. Brush on more cement, smooth it out, and let it set at least overnight before checking the repair for strength.

Wiring Checks

After you get the case open, look for broken or loose wiring. If you find any loose connections, tighten them up, and then recheck to see if this repairs the drier. If not, then check to be sure that there is power getting to the unit through the line cord. Most connections will be made with wirenuts. Take these off so that you can get to the ends of the line cord. Clip your test lamp in place and check by turning the switch on. If the lamp lights when the cord is plugged in and if the switch is operating correctly, shake the line cord to make sure that it does not have an intermittent connection.

If the motor will not run when the switch is turned *on*, check to see if there is power getting through the switch. If the motor hums but will not operate, it is a good indication of a frozen motor, due to the lack of oil. Turn the fan blade with your fingers to be sure that it can turn freely. In many instances, bobby pins and other objects have been dropped into the case and jammed the fan. Spin the fan and see. If the motor runs, but turns very slowly with a lot of buzz and hum, it may need oiling. Put about two drops on each bearing while the motor is running. If this is the trouble, you will hear the motor pick up speed right away. In some cases the motor frame may be out of line so that the bearings are binding the shaft. See that the bolts are tight, and then tap the frame with a screwdriver. This will jar the frame and line up the bearings, which are made of small brass balls held in a steel spring-clip. Tapping the frame aligns them with the shaft. You will seldom find this, but it can happen.

Brush Motors

Most of the hair driers have the simple synchronous motors, but some have the more powerful *brush* type. They are small models of the large motors used on washers, and they have wound rotors, a commutator, and brushes to transfer the power to the rotor. Fig. 5-2 shows the brushes on this type of motor. If you will look closely,

Fig. 5-2. Illustrating the brushes and commutator.

you can see one of the brushes and its spring, sticking out of one of the ventilating holes.

Whenever one of these units is taken apart, you should check the brushes for length. If they are worn down to about ¼ inch, replace them. Take one of the old brushes with you to the electrical supply store, so that you will be sure to get the right length and, above all, the right size. A too-long brush can be cut off, but one that is too big must be painstakingly sanded down to fit, by rubbing it on a piece of sandpaper on a flat surface. Be very sure that the brushes fit snugly in the holders, but still slip freely back and forth. If necessary, the old springs can be used on the new brushes. Be sure that they have not lost their tension from being overheated. The end of the clip is lifted carefully up and the brush and holder slides out. In other models, the insulated holder is attached to the motor, and the brush held in by an insulated cap screwed into the end of the holder. Check the wires to the holder, if they are exposed, make sure that they are not bare or have worn insulation.

Cleaning Commutators

On one end of the rotor you will see a cylinder made of brass bars, this is the *commutator*, which makes the electrical connections to the wound rotor. If the brushes have worn down too far, they will arc, and this will make the commutator very rough and dirty. Fig. 5-3 shows the commutator of the motor, after disassembly. Note how rough it looks. Many commutators will look dark, but this does not indicate damage; as long as the surface is smooth and shiny, a dark brown color is normal. Professional servicemen clean commutators while they are running; this is not recommended for the amateur. Take the motor apart. You can see the two or three bolts holding it together. Take the brushes out, and carefully lift the outer housing off the armature.

Cut a strip of very fine sandpaper about the width of the commutator bars. Wrap it around the commutator and turn the armature in your hand. In most cases it will not take long to get it cleaned and as smooth and shiny as the one in Fig. 5-4. If the motor is very old, you may see a groove worn around the bars by the brushes. This

Fig. 5-3. A view of the motor commutator.

Fig. 5-4. A view of the commutator after cleaning.

is not necessarily bad, but if the groove is deep enough, you may have to replace the armature. Shorted or open coils in the armature will cause a very heavy sparking *at one place;* usually two or three bars will be very badly pitted from the arcing. This means replacement of the armature, for there is no way to fix it, aside from having it rewound. A new one is much cheaper.

Running-In New Brushes

When new brushes are installed, they must be "run-in." This means running the motor until the end of the new brush is worn off so that it fits smoothly to the surface of the commutator. A good brush should be slightly concave on the end and very smooth and shiny. (A rough or pitted brush, or one showing uneven wear, has been bouncing and arcing; check the spring tension and the commutator surface.) You can speed up the run-in by sanding the end of the brush to a concave contour before installation. Wrap sandpaper around a cylindrical object (a pencil, for example), and run the brush back and forth a few times. When you are installing the brush, be sure that the concave surface is set correctly on the commutator and not crosswise.

Be sure that the brushes are free in the holders. Now, start the motor. You will probably see a good deal of sparking at the commutator during the first couple of minutes, but this should stop as the brush fits itself to the commutator. A normal motor will have a few very small sparks at each brush while running. A hot, blue spark, going almost all the way around the commutator, means a bad brush or a bad commutator, and something is seriously wrong. This, by the way, will make a very loud noise in a radio and tear up a television picture. When reassembling the motor, be sure that the brushes are *out;* put them in only after the motor has been put back together. Spin the fan to make sure that the rotor is free. If the motor has an odd method of brush mounting, etc., make a little scratch-paper sketch of how things look and where they go, *before* tearing it down. This can save you a lot of trouble when putting it back together.

Switches

Switches are responsible for a lot of troubles. If the motor will not run or the heater is cold, check the line cord and then check the switch. If it is intermittent—that is, it turns on one time then refuses to operate the next—and it is not very dirty, it may be all right after cleaning. The easiest way to clean it is to spray a cleaning compound into the body of the switch; this is available at radio supply stores under the name of *contact cleaner.* Spray it well, then work the switch several times; then recheck the switch. If it still does not work after this, replace it.

All of these machines use some kind of selector switch, as we said earlier. Some have separate switches for fan and heater, with the heater current going through the fan switch so that the heater cannot be turned on until the fan is running. Others have rotary or even push-button switches. Many switches have molded markings, etc., that will help you identify the terminals. If you wish, you can tie little tags to the wires, numbered 1,2,3, etc., or mark the switch itself with a soft pencil or crayon—anything that will help you remember the correct hookup.

If a motor has two identical wires, as many of them do, it does not make any difference "which goes where," as long as they are on the motor terminals. If you do want to identify one of them, tie a knot in the end or put a small piece of surgical tape around it. You can wrap common surgical tape around a wire and write a number on it.

Fig. 5-5 shows a rotary selector switch used on another model. This one is operated by an arm, shown coming out below the switch to the right. The plastic body, holding the contacts, is fastened to the top by two small metal hooks and arms. To get this off, carefully bend the hooks back with the end of a screwdriver as shown.

Fig. 5-5. Viewing one type of selector switch.

Fig. 5-6 shows how this type of switch looks after the top is removed. The Z-shaped metal parts in the top are the contacts, and a rotary selector unit fits in the center. This has a D-shaped hole, which fits over a flat on the shaft. Check the surfaces of the contacts to make sure that they are clean and bright. This is a common trouble in this kind of switch; look for loose wires at the contacts. Sometimes all but a strand or two of the wire will break. The contacts can be lifted out of the slots, and the wire soldered back. Remove from the contact, any blobs of solder which will prevent the switch from mounting back in the slot. On this model, the switch arm has a small plastic knob; this must be removed before the top of the case can be removed. A small "blade" is mounted on the knob. This slips into a slot in the end of the switch arm itself. To remove the knob, pull straight out from the switch. If it will not come off, check to make sure that there is not a setscrew that must be loosened first. Be sure to take the knob off before you try to put the case back together.

The drier shown in Fig. 5-2 has a rotary selector switch of a different type. Fig. 5-7 shows a front view of this switch. The large metal plate around the shaft is the main switch body, and the tiny "tips"

Fig. 5-6. Showing a detailed view of the selector switch.

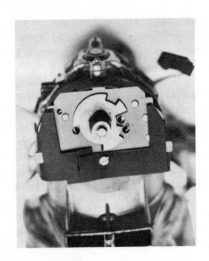

Fig. 5-7. Exterior view of rotary selector switch used on drier shown in Fig. 5-1.

seen coming through the holes in the insulator-plate are the actual contacts. The switch is shown in the off position. Starting at the top and going clockwise, the first contact is "motor only," the second, "motor plus low heat," and the third, "motor plus both heaters" (high).

Note that after the rotor passes the motor contact it stays in contact with the motor contact unil it gets all the way back to the off position again. If this kind of switch gives trouble, the little contact "points" can be bent back or worn off so that they will not touch the rotor. They can usually be bent back up so that they do make contact. Some of the small machines use slide switches. These are often pretty delicate and do not last too long. If one of these gives trouble, replace it. New switches like it can be found at radio supply stores.

Thermostats

Thermostats should be included with switches, because they are nothing but automatic switches, and they have the same troubles. A detailed discussion of thermostats will be found in the section on electric heaters. In hair driers the thermostat is usually mounted on the heating element itself. Its purpose is to cut the heater off if it gets too hot or if the fan should stop. These have contacts just like some rotary switches; if they get dirty, they can be cleaned. Do not bend the bimetal blade, because this will upset the temperature setting of the thermostat and it may not open at the right temperature. In some makes this may be hooked up so that it cuts off the fan or the complete unit if the drier gets too hot.

Heaters

Generally all machines use the "open-wire" type element, mounted on a little mica card. These are mounted inside the air duct so that the air stream blows over the unit. Small metal eyelets are used to make the connections, because the heater wire cannot be soldered. The wire leads are often fastened securely to the heater element itself, and all connections and disconnections must be made from the other end. After long use, the wires get brittle from repeated heating and cooling, and they may break. If they are open, they are easy to see. There is no practical way of repairing the element. You may find a general-replacement type of element, but be sure to take the old one with you so that you can match them up. Since they must fit in the small space inside the air duct, the new element must be an exact duplicate of the original one. New elements are not expensive, so replacement is better than trying to repair one.

The elements are usually made in pairs, with one smaller than the other. For low heat, the smallest one is turned on. For medium heat, the larger one. For high heat, both are on at once. This accounts for the construction of the selector switches.

Fans

There are two kinds of fans; the plastic disc with fins and a metal disc with blades, usually spot-welded on. About the only fan trouble you will find will be the ones that are loose on the shaft—they rattle while the motor is running. This type is usually held on with a setscrew through the hub, which is generally an *Allen* or inside-hex setscrew. You will need a special, long, *Allen* wrench to get to the shaft. This can be found at auto supply and radio stores, in kits of several sizes.

In the plastic fan a rectangular slot is molded in the back and is held on the shaft by a *Tinnerman* nut. A *Tinnerman* nut is made from a piece of stamped spring-steel, with "ears" on either side of the center hole. These are simply pushed on over the end of a round stud or screw and held by spring tension. To remove one, pry the ears up with a sharp-pointed tool, and pry it straight up and off. After removing the nut, push the ears back down flat again; to replace, simply push it back on tightly. You will find these used in other places on some driers to hold parts, etc. If one of the spot-welds on a metal fan breaks, it will rattle while running. Some of them can be soldered, but this could unbalance the blade. A better repair is a thin layer of expoxy resin cement on either side of the break. This is much lighter than solder and it usually holds just as well. Be sure to let this cement dry overnight before the drier is run again.

In the case of the stamped-out sheet-metal fans, if the hub has come loose from the blades, it will rattle. These are often quite difficult to solder. However, the epoxy cement will make a good repair for such troubles. Run a bead of the cement around the hub, on each side, and turn the hub with your fingers so that the cement works inside the joint. Let it dry overnight, and the fan will be as good as new. If the fan makes a horrible noise when it is running, it is probably hitting something. The thin sheet-metal case could be bent or there could be a bobby pin inside. Take it apart and check. If it is hitting something, you will be able to see the marks inside the fan housing. Turn the fan with your fingers, and you will be able to tell what it is hitting, and clear it.

HOSES AND FITTINGS

Now we come to a difficult part as far as repairs are concerned—the plastic hoses and fittings. These hoses are very flexible, made of a thin plastic with a wire spiral inside to keep them from collapsing.

If they get too hot or are twisted too much, the spiral wire can come loose. This lets the hose collapse so that the air cannot get through, as shown in Fig. 5-8. Frankly, the best repair in a lot of cases is a new hose. In emergencies, you may be able to fix it so that it will work for a while at least. The "end fittings" of the hose are usually made of soft plastic or rubber. A slot is made around the end fittings to hold the hose to the bonnet. The hose can be taken out by carefully squeezing it and prying it up with a small screwdriver. You will not have to take both ends loose; the end at the case is enough.

Fig. 5-8. Damaged drier air hose.

Sometimes the hose will come out of the fitting, leaving it undamaged. If so, it can usually be screwed back in. When the fitting is molded onto the hose, it forms threads around the spiral wire. If the end of the hose is flattened or torn, cut it off square, clipping the wire with wire cutters and trimming the plastic with a sharp knife. Then screw it back in. A dab of plastic cement will hold it, although it will usually fit tightly enough without this. Some driers have metal fittings on the case, with threads to hold the hose. These are much easier to work with.

If the hose has collapsed, take one end off, and carefully push a smooth rod through it. Fig. 5-9 shows a hose with a broomstick pushed through it, a good fit for a large-size hose. If your hose is smaller than this, you may have to use a round curtain rod, golf-club shaft, or any smooth rod that will just slide inside. This holds the hose open so that you can work on it. Now very carefully work the metal spiral back into place. Hold the plastic tightly with one hand and work the turns of the wire back with the end of your thumb until the spirals are in their original position. The spirals may not be perfect, but they will hold the hose open so that air can get through.

The condition of the hose will tell whether this repair will last or not. If the hose is torn or the wires are badly bent, it may not. In many cases, after getting the wires straightened, you can warm the hose with a heat lamp and the plastic will tighten up. You cannot get inside to apply cement to the turns of wire, of course.

Fig. 5-9. Repairing collapsed air hose.

but you can touch the hose very lightly with the tip of a hot soldering iron, and melt it just a little so that the plastic will hold the wire in place. If the hose is split or broken, it will be hard to fix. However, in emergencies you can wind vinyl-plastic electrician's tape around the damaged portion. The ¼-inch tape makes for a neater job, but you can use the standard ½-inch tape and split it down the center with scissors or a very sharp knife. Cut this tape in strips about 8 to 10 inches long. Warm it over a gas burner or lighter and it will get very soft and pliable. It can be wound over the hose to seal the split or hole. Use two layers of tape, one wound each way, and do not pull the tape too tightly, for this will make the hose collapse.

Many hoses are made of vinyl plastic. For these hoses, a patching kit, like those sold for repairing plastic toys, will do a good job. Small pieces of transparent vinyl come with the kits, with a supply of plastic cement. Coat the patch with the cement, put it on, and let it dry at least overnight for maximum strength.

Cases and Fittings

The cases, as we said, are made of soft thermoplastic material. This means a plastic that softens when hot, then hardens again. These will often deform under the heat from the heating element, especially around the hose outlet. If the ends are ragged, trim them off with a sharp knife and fit the end back into the case as tightly as possible. Now, with a soldering-iron tip or heated spatula, melt the plastic until it fits together. Fill up the holes with bits of scrap, melting them with the spatula and smoothing them down as well as possible. If there are any large holes left, patch them with short bits of vinyl tape.

This kind of a job can often be made easier by using the epoxy resin cement. Smooth it into and over the fitting, let it dry overnight, and it will hold longer than the original joint. You can make patches with bits of tape, pasting them in place with the epoxy and making a tight joint. If there is any way to make this joint to a metal part, it will be better. You may be able to find, or make up, a piece of thin sheetmetal out of a spice-can or something like it, that will fit snugly into the metal housing of the heater, and help make a tight joint. The metal "tube" made from the sheetmetal must be the right size to fit snugly *inside* the hose. With the end of the tube cut square, snip small slits lengthwise. Bend every other one of these out, and you will make a "flange" that will catch the end of the tube in the hole. If the case is iron or steel, it can be soldered in place, but if it isn't, you can cement it in with epoxy and it will hold just as well. If you are lucky, you can find a can that will be a good fit, and you can trim and bend it to make locking lugs that will slip through the notches in the hole and turn to lock in place.

After this has set up, slip the end of the hose over it. If it is just a little bit loose, snap about three small rubber bands around the hose; these will hold it tightly in place on the end of the tube. It can also be cemented in place, or held by softening long strips of vinyl tape and wrapping them around the end of the hose, over the tube. Cut the end of the hose square and make sure that there are not any holes or breaks in it which would leak air. As a very last resort, you can use a small hose clamp, like those used on cars to hold radiator hoses. The "endless-screw" type with a thin metal band will hold very tightly, but it isn't too pretty.

6

Electric Massage Machines

There are several different types of electric massage units. Some fasten to the back of your hand with straps, and others with plastic cases have a smooth aluminum plate which is applied to the skin. Most machines are similar in that they have some sort of electrical unit which makes the machine vibrate at a fairly high speed to give a soothing massage when the hand or plate is rubbed over the skin. Some have built-in heating units. The first versions of these machines are still used in some models. They have a very small electric motor which has an eccentric weight on the shaft that acts like an unbalanced flywheel. As the motor turns, this causes the vibration. In the other type, a simple coil with an iron bracket is used.

The unit shown in Fig. 6-1 provides vibration for massage and heat. A selection switch (shown with the knob removed) allows the choice of massage: vibration only, massage with heat, and heat without vibration. The aluminum disc below the unit is applied to the skin. It is held in place by two long screws which are recessed so that they cannot touch the skin and scratch. The heating element used in this is very simple; it is a 3500-ohm resistor rated at 10 watts; it can be seen inside the round opening in the case. It is mounted very close to the aluminum disc, but not touching it. In use, the resistor is connected directly across the a-c line and will dissipate about 4.0 watts, due to its high resistance. This does not sound like much, but it will make the disc comfortably warm in use.

If this unit should burn out, you can get a new resistor at any radio-television supply house. These are standard television parts used in service work. Be sure to get exactly the same size and wattage as is stamped on the body of the resistor. The vibrator unit shown in Fig. 6-2 is a very simple machine. A coil is mounted on a "C-shaped" spring, and this holds it near a small plate of iron. When alternating current is applied to the coil, it generates a "moving magnetic field" which is constantly changing. This field alternately pulls the coil closer and pushes it away from the iron plate, 60 times a second. Since the coil has a fairly heavy iron core, the resulting movement causes the whole unit to vibrate. The advantage of this type of vibrator is that there are no switch contacts used; the moving magnetic field does all the changing.

The unit is mounted in a plastic case, and all parts are held in place by self-tapping screws. These go into holes, studs, etc. in the case as you can see in Fig. 6-2. The coil and heating resistor are mounted on a thin phenolic disc, which can be seen in Fig. 6-1. Four screws around the rim hold the disc into the case. The case is split into two halves held together by more screws. The selector switch is held in place by a large, thin nut which can be removed with a wrench or pliers if the switch needs replacement. The control knob

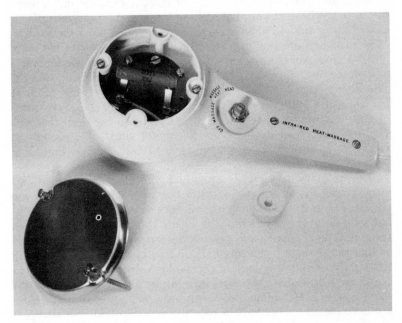

Fig. 6-1. Heat-massage unit with aluminum plate removed to expose heating unit.

slips onto the shaft, which is split to give enough tension to hold the knob. If the knob becomes loose, carefully pry the ends of the shaft apart; this will give it a tighter grip. In other models, the knob may be held by a very small setscrew. This must be loosened before the knob can be removed.

Electrical repairs to this kind of unit are simple. There are only two parts: the vibrator coil and heating resistor. Check to see which one is not working—the heater or vibrator. If neither works, check

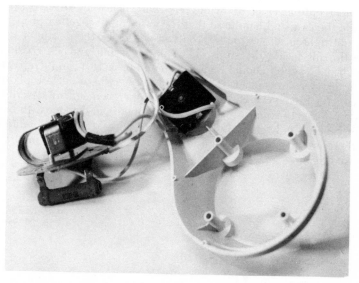

Fig. 6-2. Exposed vibrator unit of the massage machine.

the line cord to make sure that power is getting to the machine. The neon test-lamp is very handy for this. One quick check of the line cord, switch, and plug is to turn the switch to *heat*, and check for voltage with the neon tester. Insert the test prods across the terminals of the resistor, which are exposed when the aluminum disc is removed. If you get voltage here, the cord is in operating condition. Leave it turned on for about 15 seconds. If the resistor is good, you will be able to feel the heat by putting a fingertip near it. The resistor is *wirewound* and covered with an insulating compound which is very hard. These resistors are very durable, but occasionally you will find one which is cracked, or corroded, and will be open. They can be easily replaced. The resistor does not get hot enough to melt solder, so they can be soldered in place.

To get the case apart, remove the two screws in the handle, and the two inside the opening of the case. Pry the halves of the case very carefully apart, being careful not to pull any of the wires loose. If the resistor becomes warm, but the coil will not vibrate, it may be open. Check for voltage across its terminals to make sure, using the neon light. The switch may get dirty and make intermittent contacts on the two functions. Try spraying some contact cleaner on the switch and turning it back and forth several times. Check the wires to make sure that none of them are loose.

When you put the case back together, make sure that none of the wires is outside; see that both halves fit snugly together without any perceptible crack showing. The wires must be dressed down inside the case and handle so that the case can fit together properly. Do not tighten screws too tightly; you will crack the plastic or strip the threads inside the studs. This plastic is fairly shock resistant, but, if the machine should be dropped and broken, it can be repaired with epoxy resin cement. If the case is an acrylic or acetate plastic, it can be fixed very easily with the proper cement, as described earlier. Since this unit is used around the body, in contact with bare skin, be especially careful to keep the line cord in perfect condition. If there are any breaks in the insulation, replace the cord before it is used again.

7

Electric Shoe Polishers

Electric shoe polishers are very useful things. Besides shining shoes, they can be used for other things such as shining the furniture, silver, trophies, and brasswork. In addition to a small battery-operated handheld model, there are several a-c-powered types, also handheld, and a small floor-model. The floor model is intended to be fastened to a solid surface and has a dual-shaft motor, with a brush or buffer on each end. The battery-operated type, as shown in Fig. 7-1, uses four Type D flashlight cells in series and a 6-volt d-c motor. The motor drives a small gearbox, with reduction-gearing to slow the speed down and give more power. Motors of this type are completely sealed and cannot be taken apart for repair. The gearbox is underneath the motor and can be taken apart by removing the *Phillips* screws. These are accessible from inside the case. This is a molded plastic case, and snaps apart for battery replacement; the case latches can be seen on the ends.

The major difficulties with this model are weak or dead batteries and dirty battery contacts. The two flat springs seen on the motor bracket make contact with the batteries, and the contact plate on the other end completes the circuit. Make sure that the springs have plenty of tension so that they make good contact and hold the batteries tightly. If a set of batteries is allowed to run down inside the case, they may leak. The resulting corrosion may eat up the battery contact arms. If this happens, the fastest way to repair it is to make up a set of new arms out of thin brass stock, and rivet or solder them in place.

If the contact points (where the battery terminals touch the arms) are roughened or corroded, clean them with fine sandpaper until

they are bright and shiny. You can give each one a very thin coat
of petroleum jelly (*Vaseline*) by rubbing a greasy fingertip over it;
this will help keep the metal from corroding in the future. For best
results, remember to take the batteries out of the case when storing
it for any length of time. The switch is a slide type, seen on the
lower part of the case near the motor. The switch can develop poor
contact and fail. If so, spray some contact cleaner into it, and work

Fig. 7-1. Battery-operated shoe polisher with case opened.

it back and forth several times. If this does not clean the switch, you
will have to replace it. These slide switches can be found at any
radio-television supply house. Get an "spst" (single-pole, single
throw) type.

The a-c–powered handheld units work in the same way, but are
more powerful and elaborate. Like the others, they have molded
plastic cases, held by several *Phillips* screws. Fig. 7-2 shows a typical
unit with the top half of the case removed. The motor is in the center. It drives a gearbox, with a worm and pinion gear, seen at the
left of the motor. This drives a small, toothed, rubber belt, which in
turn drives the chuck where the brushes, buffers, etc. are inserted.
The inside of the chuck has right-hand threads, of a fairly high
pitch, as you can see from the brush and polish applier below the
unit. The chuck turns counterclockwise so that the brushes will not
unscrew during operation.

The brushes in the motor are fitted between a pair of plastic discs,
seen just to the left of the motor in the close-up of Fig. 7-3. A pair
of small coil springs are mounted between the discs; one end presses

Fig. 7-2. Handheld a-c–powered shoe polisher.

on the brush for tension, and the other is hooked into a terminal lug on the disc for electrical contact. To replace the brushes in this motor, take out the three black-headed *Phillips* screws holding them in the case. This will allow the motor and gear case to be lifted up and out of the case so that you can get to the brushes, which are on the lower part. The belt will have to be taken off to allow the motor to come up high enough.

Fig. 7-4 is a closeup of the belt-drive and chuck assembly. The front-end mounting is a small square block with the chuck and pulley. This fits into a slot in the end of the case. To change the belt, lift this block up and out of the slot, and remove the belt. Replacement belts are available at your appliance dealer. A part number is stamped on the belt, but if the number is illegible, take the old belt along so that you will be sure to get the right length. The gearcase itself should give little trouble. A metal worm on the end of the motor shaft drives a nylon pinion, which in turn drives

Fig. 7-3. Motor, switch, and gearcase of an electric shoe polisher.

71

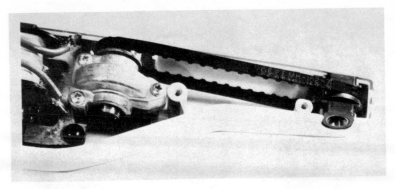

Fig. 7-4. Gearcase and drive belt assembly.

a toothed plastic pulley, as you can see in the close-up of Fig. 7-5. The gearcase is sealed and should need lubrication only after very long intervals. It should be filled with a cream grease, like that sold at radio supply stores under the name *Lubriplate*. In some cases, the front bearing and pulley may need a drop or two of light oil if they bind or drag.

All of the working parts are mounted in one half of the case. The unit can be run, with the top half of the case off. When putting the case back together, be very careful; do not insert any of the screws

Fig. 7-5. Close-up view of the gearcase.

until you have fitted the two halves tightly together. The motor wires run from the switch to the motor terminals. A small sheet-metal bracket with grooves in each end is mounted over the small cooling fan to keep the plastic-covered wires from getting down into the fan. This would jam the motor or, worse still, cause the fan to cut through the insulation of the wires and cause a short. Be sure that they are fitted in the grooves, to keep them out of trouble.

As with all other plastic-case appliances, be very careful when replacing the screws; do not run them up too tightly. Self-tapping screws are used, cutting their own threads in the soft plastic, and these can be stripped out if you use too much force. Once they are stripped, it is hard to get them to hold again. You can, in emergencies, fill the hole with plastic cement, and run the screw in very lightly. Let this set overnight at least, and then tighten the screw. Broken cases can be repaired as mentioned before. Epoxy cement will hold any of them or, if you can identify the plastic used, you can get the proper cement at a radio supply house or appliance dealer.

If the motor refuses to run in either direction, check the switch first. You can check to see if there is actually any voltage on the motor by touching the neon tester prods to the a-c line terminal and either one of the motor terminals on the switch. If the neon tester lights, there is voltage on the switch, and the motor has continuity (there are no broken wires). If the tester lights on one terminal, but not on the other, that field winding is probably open. You can check the switch, to see if it is making good contact, by pushing it closed with one hand, and then touching the test prods to the closed terminals. You should not see even a flicker of the lamp; if you do, it means that the contacts are dirty.

To make a definite check of the switch, you can, *very* carefully, short between the "AC" and "F" with the tip of a small screwdriver blade. This should close the circuit and make the motor run forward. It is the same thing for reverse. Be sure to use a well-insulated screwdriver, and keep your fingers well away from any metal on the blade. All of the terminals are *hot* when the plug is inserted in the outlet. If the lamp will not light across the switch terminals, one of the brushes may be stuck or worn off so far that it will not make contact with the commutator. You can see the brushes between the discs, and move them with a toothpick, matchstick, or similar rod. You can use a very small screwdriver, but if you do, be very sure that the line plug is pulled out of the outlet!

If the motor hums, but will not run, pull the plug, and try to turn the cooling fan with a small screwdriver. There should be a little "drag" due to the worm-gearing, but the motor should not be too tight. This will tell you whether the motor is stuck or not. If there seems to be too much drag, take the cover off the gearbox, and check to see if it is dry, with no lubricant at all. If the motor runs, but the belt does not move, the small plastic pinion in the gearbox may have lost some teeth. The worm gear is made of hardened steel, and the pinion of plastic. The worm never wears out, but the pinion does. It's comparatively simple to put in a new pinion gear, by simply dropping its shaft into the bearing which is exposed when you remove the gearcase lid. To replace a worm means replacing the whole motor. So, the designer makes the pinion of plastic, so that it will "take the wear." This makes a much quieter-running gear combination.

8

Photoelectric Light Controls

One of the electrical/electronic devices that have become very popular, especially in rural and suburban areas, is the *automatic yardlight*. They come in all shapes and sizes, such as, postlanterns, floodlights, spotlights, and even mercury-vapor types like those used for street lighting. The mercury-vapor lights can illuminate large areas when they are mounted on high poles. They all use the same kind of control unit—a photoelectric cell which is exposed to the outside light. When this falls below a preset light level, the lamp turns on. The same type of mechanism is used in many cities to control streetlights, electric signs, and similar devices.

Fig. 8-1 shows the schematic of a typical unit. This is one of the smaller types which is mounted on top of a reflector, and uses bulbs with ratings up to 300 watts. Here, the a-c current comes in at the top (white) wire, flows through a 5100-ohm resistor (R) through a cadmium-sulphide cell (abbreviated CdS), then through the relay coil, and back to the line. The CdS cell in this application is a "variable resistor." The wiggly arrows denote the fact that the resistance is determined by the amount of *light* which falls on the surface. When it is dark, the cell has a high resistance; when light falls on it, the resistance goes down, allowing more current to flow. The actual control of the lamp bulb is done by the contacts of the sensitive relay. These contacts are normally closed, meaning that when the relay has no current through it, the spring holds the contacts closed and the light is on.

When light falls on the photocell, its resistance goes down and more current flows through the relay; its coil is energized and pulls the contacts open, extinguishing the lamp. This gives the device a "fail-safe" operation—if anything goes wrong with the control circuits, the lamp will stay on all the time. Fig. 8-2 shows the photoelectric control unit with cover removed. The relay is at the right, and the rectangular plastic-covered object at the top is the CdS photocell. The flat, light-colored object is the resistor, and the capacitor is alongside it. The reflector can be seen under the unit. The contact points of the relay are at the bottom, and the spring can be seen on top of the coil. In normal operation, a dome-shaped cover is placed over the unit and a small, round window allows light to reach the photocell. Most manufacturers recommended that this be installed so that the window faces north. This keeps the direct rays of the sun from striking the photocell and gives more accurate control of operation.

To check one of these units, replace the lamp with one known to be good. Then cover the photocell window with the palm of your hand; you should be able to hear the relay click. If nothing happens, turn the power off, and take off the cover. There will be several hot wires exposed when the cover is removed, and you will probably be standing on a ladder, so do not take any chances. Check the relay contacts. If these are dirty, burned, or pitted, they may not be making good contact. In most of these units, the relay contacts will be easily accessible, as shown in Fig. 8-2. Pull a strip of fine sandpaper between the contacts to clean them and make sure that the spring has enough tension to pull them firmly together. Look for signs of visible damage. If lightning has struck anywhere near the area, there is always the possibility of damage. It will leave definite traces, through burned resistors or charred parts and smoked places where the current has flashed across insulation, etc. If this has happened, remove the unit for repairs.

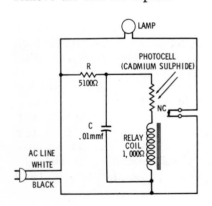

Fig. 8-1. Schematic diagram of a small
photoelectric cell.

Fig. 8-2. Photoelectric control unit.

If there are no visible signs of damage, use an insulated tool, like a plastic rod, wooden dowel, etc., and turn the power back on, being *very* careful not to touch any of the exposed terminals. Using the insulated tool, very gently push the relay contacts together. If the lamp lights, then this much is operating properly. Next, cover the photocell with a pad of dark cloth, cardboard, etc. This should make the relay armature move. In this circuit, it should open the armature, allowing the contacts to close, and turning the lamp on. If the relay armature does not move, then the unit will have to be removed for an electrical checkup. (Be sure to turn the power off first.) This will require a small volt-ohmmeter, because the resistance of the complete circuit must be checked. Check the total resistance across the a-c line terminals. All of these resistance measurements must be made with *both* wires disconnected from the a-c line. The resistor, as shown, should read 5100 ohms, the relay coil about 1000 ohms, and the photocell between 2000 and about 15,000 ohms, depending on the amount of light falling on it.

Cover the face of the cell and take a resistance reading directly across the terminals. The "dark-reading" should be high. Uncover the cell and let the bench light strike it, the resistance should drop to about 1500–2000 ohms. If all of these readings are correct, the unit should work. Most of these units use a small capacitor (C) across the relay coil and photocell as a filter. If this should be shorted, the relay will not work and the 5100-ohm resistor may be burned up as well. Check the total resistance across the capacitor terminals. This should be the sum of the resistances of the photocell and the relay coil, as in Fig. 8-1. For example, if the cell is covered, you should read about 15,000 ohms. If the capacitor is shorted, you may read 100 to 200 ohms or even a dead short (zero resistance). To make a reliable test, disconnect one end of the capacitor, and recheck the resistance. You should never read any resistance between the leads of a good capacitor. It should be a completely open circuit. If the capacitor is shorted, remove it and take it to a radio-television shop, they can tell you what size it was, by its color code. If this is not decipherable, a 0.01-mfd capacitor at 600 working volts, is a pretty good compromise value, since it is the most common size found in such circuits.

In the unit shown in Fig. 8-2, you can get at the working parts for replacement by taking the socket off, then the reflector. These are held by screws inside the reflector. The control unit is held in place by two long screws; the heads of these can be seen next to the relay coil. They will not come out from this side; there are two nuts on each screw on the underside. These can be taken off after the socket and reflector have been removed. This uses a printed-circuit type of board, with all of the solder connections on the under side.

Fig. 8-3 shows the schematic of a larger unit. Although it is exactly like the first in principle, it has some refinements. It is used

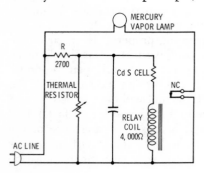

Fig. 8-3. Schematic diagram of a large
photoelectric cell.

to control heavy-duty mercury-vapor lamps like those used for street lighting or for large area lighting in rural areas. This is a plug-in unit; complete control unit can be removed by turning it slightly to the left (counterclockwise) and then pulling it up and out of its socket. Fig. 8-4 shows the construction. Note the similarity to the first unit. Relay contacts are larger, so that they can handle the

Fig. 8-4. Heavy-duty photoelectric control unit.

heavier currents. A temperature-compensating resistor is mounted across coil and photocell. The "wing-shaped" devices seen at the right are overlapping *Polaroid* plastic shutters. These can be adjusted so that only the desired amount of light strikes the photocell. This photocell is a CdS cell exactly like the first unit, but is mounted in a cylindrical case, just left of the shutters.

The control unit in Fig. 8-1 works almost instantly. There is usually about a 1-second delay between light striking the photocell and the lamp turning on. In the larger unit of Fig. 8-3, there will be a slightly longer delay. This is not due to the control unit, but to the characteristics of a mercury-vapor lamp. The mercury-vapor lamp is an arc lamp, and it takes a second or two for it to build up enough voltage to "strike." This delay will not be noticeable in normal operation, but if there is a violent thunderstorm with fairly constant lightning flashes, you may notice the lamp going off, on, then off again erratically. After a particularly brilliant flash, it may go off and stay off for quite a while. The photocells can be temporarily "blocked" by large amounts of light, just as the human eye can be momentarily blinded. However, this will not damage anything, unless the lamp is actually hit by lightning.

9

Portable Table Ovens

There is one appliance which has become very popular in the past few years. This well-deserved popularity is due to its convenience; it makes meal preparation much easier. There are several different names for these, but most people seem to use the shortest one, *table ovens*. They are, generally, simple—a small metal cabinet with insulating plastic feet. Inside, a metal tray or grille, or a combination of both, holds the food. An electric radiant-heating element is mounted in the top. These ovens can be used for broiling, toasting, baking, thawing and heating frozen foods, and many other purposes, right on the dining table.

Fig. 9-1 shows one of the heating elements and an inside view of the cabinet. Some of the more elaborate types have insulated cabinets, and even the smallest have dual thicknesses of metal on all sides. The most common heating element is the spiral-wire type shown here; some of the units use the same sealed-unit type of heating elements used in electric ranges. The spiral-wire type uses *Nichrome* wire stretched over ceramic supports. The supports slip into notches stamped out of the inner liner, and the tension of the spring element holds them in place.

The heating element is attached to a two-prong plug on the cabinet. The two prongs of the connector are mounted on a small tab stamped out of the cabinet. This one uses a pair of ceramic blocks as insulators, one on either side of the metal. The holes in the metal are made large enough to let shoulders on the insulators fit snugly inside. This keeps the metal prongs from touching the metal of the case, which would cause a short or dangerous shock hazard. A

Fig. 9-1. Inside view of a typical portable table oven, showing the spiral-wire heating elements.

shoulder on the prongs fits against the outside of the insulator, and the inner end is threaded. Nuts and washers are used to hold the resistance wire. The wire is twisted around the "screw," and a metal washer is used to keep it in place and the nut tightened. The rest of the wire is cut off or twisted around the element to keep it from shorting to the other elements. The inside of these units uses a highly polished metal surface to reflect the heat onto the food being cooked.

Fig. 9-2 shows an exterior view of the connector prongs and another way of mounting them on the metal case. Here, the prongs are insulated by thick mica washers on each side. The inner ones have shoulders which fit inside the hole to keep the prongs centered. Flat washers are used on the outside, with flat metal washers on each side, so that the fragile mica will not be damaged by tightening the mounting nuts. As you can see, the base of each prong is made in the shape of a nut with hexagonal stamping, so that a nutdriver type of wrench can be used to hold the outer end while the nuts are tightened on the inside. Two nuts are used on each: The first holds the prong tightly to the case, and the outer one holds the heating-element wires to the prong for electrical contact.

These prongs *must* be very tight so that they cannot slip to one side and short to the metal case. If they loosen, retighten them,

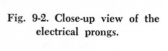

Fig. 9-2. Close-up view of the electrical prongs.

making sure that all of the insulating washers or ceramic insulators are set in the holes properly. If the mica washers are cracked or broken or if the ceramic insulators are broken, put new ones on in their place. Do not take any chances of causing a short to the case. After making repairs to these plugs, test for shorts between the case and the a-c line, with the test lamp or neon tester. You can do this by connecting one side of the test lamp to a grounded object such as a water pipe, plugging the oven in, and touching the case with the other terminal of the test lamp. *Do not* touch the metal with your bare hand until you have made this test.

Many table ovens are equipped with thermostats to control the heat. Such a unit is shown in Fig. 9-3. A metal plate covers the odd-

Fig. 9-3. Thermostat control used on table ovens.

shaped hole in the case. A plastic knob on the thermostat shaft in the center is used to set it to the desired temperature. One lead from the plug goes directly to the heating element. The other, using heavy, asbestos-insulated wire, goes through the thermostat unit. These thermostats are replaceable and work exactly as the others discussed earlier, on other heating-type appliances. Fig. 9-4 shows how to remove the control knob on this type of unit. A small set-screw must be loosened, and the knob then comes off the shaft. If

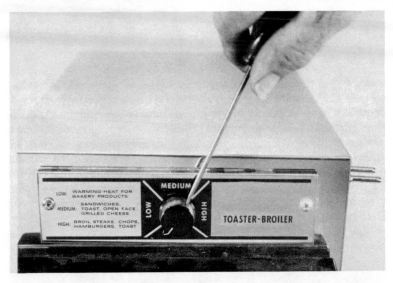

Fig. 9-4. Control panel on a typical table oven.

the knob works loose by itself, as they often do, the calibration of the thermostat will be wrong. To reset it, turn the thermostat shaft all the way counterclockwise, put the knob back on so that the arrow or indicating mark is lined up with the "low" mark on the plate, and tighten the screw again. This will work in the opposite direction, of course, if you turn the shaft all the way clockwise and, set the pointer at the "high" mark. Two small *Phillips*-head screws hold the cover plate on the case. Some of these units are pretty elaborate; they have push-button control units, built-in timers, and many other convenient features. However, they are all basically the same—a heating element plus whatever controls are used. A mechanized version of this type of appliance is shown in Fig. 9-5. The heating elements, etc. are generally the same, but a rotating spit is provided for roasting fowl and meat. A small electric motor is mounted in one end of the case to turn the spit. Push-button switches on the front panel allow the unit to be used as a rotisserie, broiler, or toaster.

Fig. 9-5. Front view of a typical rotisserie.

A thermostat holds the heat at whatever level is desired, and a built-in timer unit will make the unit run for any desired length of time and then turn itself off. Some of the more elaborate models use the same kind of electric clock control found on electric and gas ranges. When properly set, they will turn the rotisserie on at any desired time, run it for any length of time needed, and then turn it off. Some models even have a device which does not turn the heat off completely but turns it down, so that the food is kept warm until it is served.

A separate cover is fastened to one end of the main cabinet by several screws; removing these screws will let you get at the motor, thermostat, and timer unit. Heating elements in these elaborate types are often of the sealed type. They seldom give any trouble; but, if they do, they can be replaced, just like the oven and top units in an electric range. Replacement heating-elements for the spiral-wire type can be found at any hardware store, appliance dealer, or electrical-parts supply store. Fig. 9-6 shows a typical re-

Fig. 9-6. Replacement heating element.

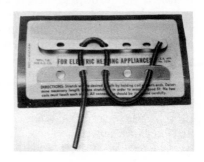

placement element on a card. This one is a 600-watt unit, as you can see from the label. Be sure to check the "rating-plate" on your appliance; the correct wattage will be stamped on this plate or stamped into the metal case of the unit. Some are 600 watts, and others will be 1000-watt types. In the units which use sealed heating elements, you will have to get an "exact-duplicate" type from the dealer for that brand of appliance, so that it will fit into the insulators properly.

When you replace one of the spiral-wire types, make sure that you get a good *clean* connection to the terminal prongs. If the inner ends of the prongs are rusted or burned, replace the prongs while you are at it. If you fail to do this, you will have a loose connection on the inside ends, and there will be arcing. This will burn up the terminals in short order and you will have the job to do over again. If an element like this has broken very close to one end, you can clean the wire, take the broken end off the terminal and fasten the unbroken section back. Make a small loop in the end of the wire so that it will make good contact with the end of the prong. You can get enough slack to make the wire reach the terminal by stretching the remaining wire a little. In an element of this kind, with a total "stretched length" of approximately 20 inches, you can break off 3 or 4 inches, and make a new connection without causing too much trouble. The element will run hotter because the remaining wire has less electrical resistance. If too much of the resistance wire is taken off, it will run so hot that it will probably burn out again in a short time.

We might get in some facts about electrical heating elements like this that are often confusing to those who have never heard the correct explanation. If we have a 600-watt heating element and we need a 300-watt one, we *do not* cut the 600-watt element in half. Instead, we *add* another 600-watt element in series with the first, so that the current has to flow through both. By hooking the two elements in series, we double the resistance so that only half as much current flows; therefore, we dissipate only half as much electrical *power.* If you want to go deeper into this fascinating subject, obtain any good textbook on basic electricity and look up "Ohm's law."

Now let's replace a spiral element. Start by making a good connection at one end. You can follow the path of the original element over the insulators by looking for the notches in their sides; the element goes into these to keep it in place. Follow the original path around the insulators until you get back to the other side of the plug. These insulators are held in place by the spring tension of the spiral element. Make sure that they are firmly in place in the notches, so that they will not come loose and let the element fall off. The elements look like springs, and they are springs, to a certain extent.

However, they will not spring back as a true spring does; once stretched too far, they will "take a set" and stay stretched. Since we *need* this tension to hold the element firmly in place, be careful. It is a good idea to follow the original path with the new element, see how it goes, and then leave only one insulator out of it, temporarily. Then fasten the loose end to the plug, and very carefully stretch the new element over that last insulator and let it snap back into place. If the element is accidentally stretched too far, so that it hangs loosely on the insulators, you can tie it to a couple of the insulators by wrapping one or two turns of bare wire around element and insulator. Twist the ends and clip them off closely. *Never* let the element or any tie wires rest so that they could touch the metal of the case.

Keep the prongs of the plug bright and clean at all times. In all heavy-current appliances, plugs and sockets tend to get dirty and corroded from arcing. Once they do get dirty, they get very hot, and arc even more. This makes them get hotter, and arc still more, and so on and on; it finally results in the replacement of the plug and socket. The plug on the cord can be taken apart and cleaned if there seems to be any trouble. Keep the connections tight. You can check them by pushing the plug onto the prongs and pulling it off again. You ought to feel a very definite "resistance" when you do this, indicating that the plug is making a good tight connection. If the plug slips on the prongs very easily, it is too loose. Tighten it up until you have to push pretty hard to get it seated. One way of avoiding unnecessary arcing when plugging or unplugging these appliances is to make sure that the current is turned *off* when the plug is put on or taken off. Plugging them in with the switch on will cause a heavy arcing, even at the line plug of the wall outlet. To turn them on and off, use the regular switch on the appliance; this is rated to carry the heavy current without excessive arcing.

The contacts on thermostats and built-in switches should be kept clean. If you hear arcing (a "frying" or raspy sound when the switch is closed), check the switch; it will probably be loose or burned enough to make poor contact. In some cases, the switch can be cleaned and tightened by bending the switch-arms slightly. If the contacts are badly burned, it is better to replace the switch. The motors used on rotisseries are small synchronous types with reduction gears to give the unit less speed and more power. Fig. 9-7 shows a typical unit. This happens to be a detachable type used with an outdoor grille or barbecue unit, but the motor and gearing are the same in most units. Note that there are no brushes; a solid rotor turns a small pinion gear, which drives a larger gear. This big gear drives another small pinion which turns the spit. The end result of this gear reduction is a speed of about 2 rpm.

Fig. 9-7. Rotisserie drive motor with case opened.

The end of the spit fits into a square hole in the final gear shaft. This can be seen in the photo of Fig. 9-8. The two bolt-heads near the chuck are used to hang this motor housing on the side of the barbecue-unit cabinet. In the table models, the motor is permanently mounted inside the cabinet. Because of the slow speed and light loading, these motors do not give too much trouble. About the only electrical trouble you will find, aside from the customary open line-cord, would be an open coil in the motor. If it will not run at all, check for a-c voltage across the coil, which is usually connected directly to the a-c line. If there is voltage at this point, check the rotor, by flipping it with a fingertip. If it is free to turn, but refuses to even try to move when the power is turned on, then the coil is open. These coils can be replaced by taking out the bolts which hold the motor frame together. The laminated frame is built in two

Fig. 9-8. Showing the square hole in the rotisserie motor which is the drive chuck.

halves; the ends of one section meet inside the motor-coil core. The frame is taken apart, the old coil removed, and then the unit is reassembled with the new one. There is no "polarity" to this kind of coil; the motor will run the same way no matter which way the coil is put on the frame.

If the rotor tries to turn and the motor hums slightly, there may be some obstruction in the gears. Being used outdoors, there is always a chance that dust or dirt has accumulated until it is heavy enough to jam the gearing. With this type of motor, which has very low starting torque, no damage will occur. It will not chew up gears as a heavier motor will; it will simply stop. The gears can be cleaned by taking the motor unit out of the housing, and washing them out with some kind of grease solvent *not gasoline*. It will not hurt if some of this gets on the motor coil, but this usually is not necessary. Any dirt or dust can be washed out of the gear unit by immersing it in the solvent in a small can or dish, and loosening the dirt with an old paintbrush.

Relubricate with some kind of light grease, such as *Lubriplate;* this will stay on the gears. Oil will drip off and be pretty messy, even if it does not get into the food. Because of the low speed, the unit will not need much lubrication in any event. There is one very common cause of trouble in this kind of equipment, as well as in any others under these circumstances—insects. If the motor unit is stored in a garage for the winter, the chances are that the all-to-common wasp called the "mud dauber" will build a *nest*. This happy little bug carries clay and makes good-sized nests, and once this clay has dried, it gets very hard, and can jam any kind of light machinery. They love ready-made holes, such as the ventilation holes in the motor case. This can cause a lot of trouble, for the thing must be taken apart and cleaned out thoroughly. The best way of avoiding this is to cover the unit completely. Store it in a tight box of some kind, or wrap it with plastic sheeting until there is no place left where the wasps can get inside. Anything with a hole bigger than ¼ inch in diameter is simply irresistible to them, so keep temptation out of their way by covering things tightly.

10

Electric Vaporizers and Bottle Warmers

There is one kind of electrical appliance that is beautifully simple; in fact, you could not get any simpler. Yet it is almost 100 percent efficient: there is absolutely no wasted energy. These are the electric vaporizers and bottle warmers. There is literally nothing to them, yet they do the job for which they are designed and do it very well. These appliances heat water. Yet they have no heating elements at all as in other heating-type appliances. How do they do it? By taking advantage of a fundamental principle of electricity —when an electric current flows through a resistance, heat is generated. This is how any electric heater works, but other units use a metallic heating element. Electric heaters of any kind are the most efficient class of machines. Heat, in all other electrical machinery, is waste. Since we *want* heat, we get a useful return for *all* of the energy we feed into it, since it is all turned into heat.

Fig. 10-1 shows how two electrodes work. In a ceramic or plastic container, the a-c line is connected to two electrodes. When we put water into the container, we complete the circuit, and current flows through the water. Water is a conducting material, but it has some electrical resistance, so heat is generated. The current will flow as long as there is water in the container. When the water has all boiled away, the device shuts itself off because the circuit is open. Practical applications of this are used for such things as warming baby bottles and heating water to make steam for vaporizing medications. Fig. 10-2 shows a home vaporizer unit. The black unit is the heating element. This fits into a well in the case and electrical contact is made

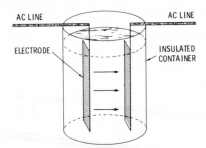

Fig. 10-1. Illustrating the use of two
electrodes used to heat water.

when it is dropped into the well. The medicine is placed inside this
unit and the case is filled with water through the small black cap
at the lower right side of the case.

Fig. 10-3 shows the heating unit. The electrodes are the two
closely spaced metal plates on the bottom. They connect to the metal
strips going up each side. Note the close spacing of the electrodes,
only about ¼ inch apart. This is done so that the water will get
hotter. The nearer the two electrodes, the greater the electric current that can flow, and the higher the temperature that can be
reached. In Fig. 10-4, you can see how the electrical circuit is ar-
ranged. The line cord comes into the case under a metal cover under
the handle, and it is fastened to two terminals with brass nuts. These

Fig. 10-2. Electric vaporizer with removable heating unit.

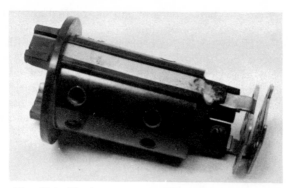

Fig. 10-3. Heating unit removed from the vaporizer.

are connected to two small screws, one on each side of the well, where they make contact with the metal strips on the sides of the electrode unit when it is placed in the well.

This unit is made removable for cleaning. Many medications used for vaporizing have a grease base. This melts and can coat the electrodes, often enough to make them waterproof if the coating is heavy enough. The unit must be cleaned out at regular intervals, so the medicine holder is made removable. In some localities, minerals in the water will leave a white deposit on the electrodes as the water boils away. Normally, this is not harmful, unless the deposit gets so thick that it threatens to cause a short circuit between the closely

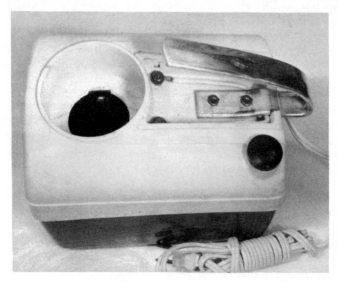

Fig. 10-4. Vaporizer with heating elements removed.

spaced electrodes. When it does, it can be scraped away. Fig. 10-5 shows a very common application of this principle—warming the baby's bottle. The outer cup is ceramic, and a ceramic disc in the bottom protects the user from any contact with the electrodes. A measured quantity of water, usually only a couple of tablespoons, is placed in the cup. When this is boiled away, the bottle is at just he right temperature, and the unit turns itself off. This suggests a timesaver for the mechanically inclined parent: he can rig up a timer which turns the unit on at a preset time; the bottle will heat up and then shut off.

Fig. 10-5. Bottle-warmer with protective ceramic disc.

The ceramic disc in the bottom is held in place by a small brass screw, but this screws in the ceramic cup, and has no electrical connection at all. The electrodes are the rectangular metal plates in the bottom of the cup. There is only one hazard in this type of unit, and that is touching the water while the unit is plugged in and filled. If you are touching a grounded object at the same time, such as a water pipe, you can get anything from a "tingle" to a fairly severe shock. However, as you can see, all of the units are designed so that it is impossible to touch the water in normal use. In the bottle-warmer, for example, the water level will be well below the small ceramic disc, so that it cannot be touched even if there is no bottle in the cup. In vaporizers the water is usually completely enclosed in the case; a plastic cover with a spout is placed over the well when the unit is being used.

The only trouble you can have with these units is a broken line cord. There are no switches and no moving parts of any kind. So, if one of these units will not work, plug it in, and check for the presence of a-c voltage at the electrodes with the neon tester or test lamp. The most common trouble, as in all units, will be a broken line cord near the plug where it gets the most bending and flexing. If you find this, replace the cord, and all will be quiet in the nursery again.

11

Vacuum Cleaners

All vacuum cleaners are generally the same in operation. From the tiny battery-powered unit no bigger than a flashlight to the large built-in home systems, each type pulls air through a hose to create a suction, which picks up dust and dirt and deposits it in a bag or container. Each has the same basic parts: a motor, a fan (usually of the modified squirrel-cage type), a duct system to channel the air flow, plus some sort of porous bag to catch the dust. In the large built-in systems the dust goes into a collector tank, but the same principle is used. Vacuum cleaners come in a very large assortment of shapes and sizes, but they generally are repaired in the same manner.

The first type of vacuum cleaners is called *upright*. It has a metal housing on wheels which holds the motor and fan, with a nozzle on the front equipped with a rotating brush to "beat" the dust out of carpets. The bag is a large cloth type mounted on a broomstick-like handle.

Other models are called *tank*-type cleaners. A metal or plastic housing holds the motor, fan and the bag, and the air is led through this by a long flexible hose, usually from ½ to 2 inches in diameter. Various attachments can be slipped onto the end of this: carpet nozzles, venetian-blind tools, and so on. A sectional-tubing handle is used for floor cleaning. Fig. 11-1 shows the basic parts of the tank-type vacuum cleaner.

The first version of the tank cleaner used a horizontal tank on skids or wheels; later models are upright, like the one in Fig. 11-1. The bag is inside the tank. Some use cloth bags, and others use disposable paper bags. There are only two parts which can go wrong in a vacuum cleaner: the electrical system, which includes the motor, line cord, plug and switch, and the air passages. Stoppage of the air flow stops the cleaner from working. If dust and dirt clog the air passages anywhere in the system, the fan can even become jammed and make you think that there is motor trouble.

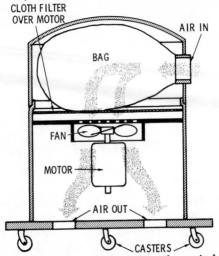

Fig. 11-1. Illustrating various sections of a typical tank-type vacuum cleaner.

The most common trouble is a lack of sufficient suction. Turn the cleaner on, and hold the palm of your hand over the suction end of the hose. It should pull your palm against the end with an audible "plunk" sound. If it does not have enough suction to do this, it will not be able to lift the dust and dirt from floors, furniture, etc. If the motor is running, but has a "labored" sound, as if it were running under a heavy load, the hose or ducts could be clogged. This will be in one of two places: the hose itself (most often) or in the housing, bag, etc. Pull the hose out of the cleaner, with the motor running. If the hose is clogged up, you will hear the motor pick up speed. Plug the end of the hose into the outlet end of the cleaner, to blow air through it in the reverse direction. This will often blow out an obstruction, and it will also blow out a great cloud of dust that lodged in the hose.

If this reverse-blow check does not clear the stoppage, get a piece of heavy wire twice the length of the hose. Double it up, and run the loop end through the hose, starting at the cleaner end. This will disloged things that may be stuck inside the hose. Such things as toothpicks, match sticks, bobby pins, and even pieces of paper can lodge at a bend in the hose. Dust and lint builds up on this obstruction, and pretty soon the hose is completely stopped up. Such things can also jam nozzles and other cleaning tools, so check them also. A simliar symptom can be heard if the bag is too full. Take the end off the tank and check it. If this is a cloth bag, empty it, and beat it well to take out the fine dust that can clog the weave of the material. If it has been in use for a long time, it is often very helpful to rinse out the bag in water, or wash it. It must be porous enough to let the air stream flow on through the material while stopping the dust.

Fig. 11-2. Dust build-up on the vacuum-cleaner motor.

Most tank cleaners have auxiliary filters which are placed ahead of the bag, to protect the motor from the finer dust particles which get through the bag. These will be cloth pads on wire rings, or plastic-foam pads which are usually fitted in the air duct so that they cover the motor. If these are not cleaned at regular intervals, they can clog up and slow down the air stream. Fig. 11-2 shows an older-type tank cleaner before this filter was cleaned. Notice how the dust has "piled up" in little "dots" over the holes in the fan housing. This is a porous paper collar which fits over the fan intake. Fig. 11-3 shows the same cleaner after it was cleaned and the filter-paper collar was replaced. This one uses a disposable paper bag which slips over the two metal rods at the right.

Fig. 11-4 shows a miniature tank cleaner with a cloth bag, with the case opened. This is a special version of the tank cleaner, made very lightweight so that it is easy to carry around. A long flexible hose and numerous attachments are used with it. The suction inlet

Fig. 11-3. A new paper-filter collar placed over the motor.

Fig. 11-4. Lightweight portable vacuum cleaner using a cloth bag.

is at the right, with the bag inside the case. The outlet is at the lower left side, under the motor. The light-colored cylinder in the center is the motor and fan housing. Note how the case is padded with fiberglass to kill the sound of the motor. The motor switch is in the end of the handle for convenience, just above the bag.

MOTOR TROUBLES

If the motor refuses to run, check the line cord and plug. This gets continually bent and pulled, and you can find many troubles in the line cord itself, near the plug. The wires may break inside the insulation. Since most of the plugs used are of the molded-on type, the only repair for this is cutting off about 3 or 4 inches of the cord, and installing a replacement-type line plug. If the jacket of the cord itself is worn, frayed, or broken in places, replace it. New cords of any length can be bought at your appliance dealer's, and this procedure is much safer. A short circuit in this cord, while it is being dragged through curtains or furniture, could be very costly.

If the cord and plug check out but the motor still will not run, check the switch. Most tank cleaners use toggle switches, on the body of the unit. Fig. 11-5 shows a typical tank-type cleaner, with the motor and fan unit taken out so that you can see where the parts

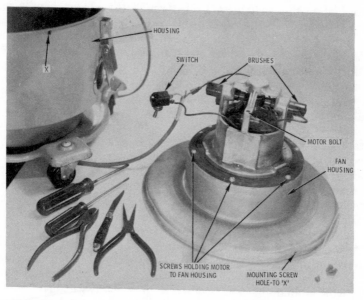

Fig. 11-5. Typical vacuum cleaner disassembled and ready for service with major parts indicated.

are located. In practically all cases, you will be able to see how the unit is held together. Turn it over and look for exposed screws around the rim, etc., that hold the top onto the base. Most of the commercial cleaners seem to employ *Phillips* screws, but some will use standard slotted screws, and some hex-head self-tapping screws. Note that the switch has attached leads, fastened to the line cord and motor wires with wirenuts. For a quick check on the switch, disconnect these, and twist the line cord and motor wire together, taking the switch completely out of the circuit. (Before you do this, be *sure* that the plug is pulled out of the wall-outlet.) Now replace the plug. If the motor starts, the switch was definitely bad.

You can often tell a lot about a switch of this type by listening to it. If it makes a sharp, clean, "click" when it is turned on, it should be operating properly. If the "click" sounds odd or is not sharp and clear, or if the toggle handle is very loose, the switch is probably bad; it will have to be replaced. Take the old switch with you, to get an exact duplicate. In almost all tank cleaners, there will be plenty of room to mount any kind of switch. In the upright cleaners and in smaller models like the cleaner of Fig. 11-4, slide switches are used. These must be replaced with *exact* duplicates, for they fit into very tight places. In fact, the slide switch in the cleaner shown fits between small lugs of the plastic case, and it must be exactly the correct size or the case will not go back together. The leads that are attached to this switch go back through the hollow handle and attach to line cord and motor leads with small wirenuts, as you can see in Fig. 11-6. The switch has been pulled out of the handle and placed on the motor so that you can see how it is hooked up.

In the upright cleaners, the switch will usually be a slide type, placed at the top of the curved part of the handle. Here, the switch is most often attached to a small chromed plate, fastened to the handle with two screws. The wires go down through the hollow handle to the motor. Once again, replacement switches must be exact duplicates to fit the close quarters. In older machines, you may find wire breakage at the bottom, where the wires come out of the handle to the motor. This is where the most bending takes place. If these wires are frayed or broken, do not try to patch or tape them. Put on new wires, and be sure that they are heavy, braid-covered, flexible types, so that they will stand the constant bending without breaking the insulation.

If the new switch has screw terminals, be sure that you get the insulation up against the switch body when you fasten the wires. Strip only about ¼ inch of wire, twist the end tightly, and wrap the wire around the loosened screw in a clockwise direction. By doing this, you will keep it from pulling out from under the screw head when you tighten it. The end of the insulation should be tight

Fig. 11-6. Slide switch used on small cleaners.

against the screw, so that there is no bare wire exposed to cause a short. In this, as in all other appliance work, be *very* sure that there is no chance of a bare wire touching the metal case or body of the appliance. This could cause a fatal shock to the user. If the cord and switch are all in good condition, check the motor itself. The most common cause of trouble is worn-out brushes. Practically all of these cleaners use brush-type motors, as you can see from the photographs. More power is developed from the brush-type motor. After a certain length of time, the brushes will wear down to the point where they do not make good contact with the commutator.

Several different types of brush fasteners are used. Most of them will have screw-caps made of insulating material, which hold the brush spring down in the holder. Others will have flat pieces of plastic, held in place by a screw. Fig. 11-7 shows a different type: The brushes are held in place by a springy strip of brass, which is fastened at one end. To remove the brush, lift the end of the strip and turn it to one side, and the brush can then be pulled out by the spring, as shown in the photo.

Most of these heavier brushes have internal "pigtails," which can be seen as a dark line inside the spring. This is to help carry the electric current and avoid overheating the spring. Be sure that the pigtail is not broken, and that the brushes are long enough. When a brush wears down to about ¼ inch, it should be replaced while

Fig. 11-7. Brush spring and holder used on vacuum-cleaner motors.

you have the motor torn down. If the commutator is dirty, clean it with a strip of sandpaper, as described previously. The commutators on these motors are large and easy to get to. A nail-board from your wife's dressing table makes a very useful brush and commutator cleaner. However, be careful not to touch any of the exposed terminals while doing this. If the nail-board is too wide to go inside the housing, clip off one side with tin-shears. The nail-board material is about the right stiffness. When the end gets worn down, clip it off, and you will have a fresh piece of sandpaper.

If there is very heavy arcing at the commutator and brushes, be sure that both brushes are long enough and free to slide in the holders. If this does not stop the arcing, check the commutator surface very carefully. If you find one or two bars which show signs of very heavy arcing (tiny yellow spots or burn marks) and pitting, and the rest of the commutator is fairly smooth, your armature is probably shorted or open between those bars. There is no practical home-remedy for this; it will have to be rewound or replaced. However, if the commutator is roughened uniformly all the way around, this could have been done by running with too-short brushes for a long period of time, or by a brush sticking in its holder. Clean the commutator very carefully, and give it a test run of about 10–15 minutes. If the brushes have not "run-in" and stopped almost all sparking by that time, *then* the armature may be bad. Do not take too much for granted; have the motor checked by a professional repairman to make sure that it is really hopeless, before you buy another armature.

HOSES

Vacuum cleaners use a flexible hose, and this has been the source of a lot of assorted troubles. They can be hard to fix. Some models used a cloth-braid–covered hose with a metal liner. Metal tubes on each end are used to connect the cleaner and the attachments. The hose often pulls out of these tubes. If it has not been flattened or torn up too badly, it can be pushed back in, and cemented in place with epoxy resin cement. If the break is close to the end, trim it off square and push it back into the fitting, applying a coat of the epoxy uniformly all the way around. Older hoses can be trimmed off with tin-shears or sometimes with a sharp hacksaw, but it can be pretty difficult.

A few cleaners use a thin plastic hose with a spiral liner, very much like the hoses on hair driers. These are subject to the same kinds of trouble: tears in the soft plastic and collapse of the spiral liner. If you are lucky, you can sometimes work the hose back into shape, or patch the tear in the plastic with cement and vinyl tape. However, the best procedure for this is replacement with a higher-grade hose.

While it is built on the same general lines as the hair drier hose, the plastic hose is heavier, and the spiral liner is wound on a much greater pitch, so that the hose is more durable. Vacuum cleaner hoses must be pretty rugged, for the cleaner is usually pulled around by the hose, and it is continually being bent and stretched. So, the hose has to be able to take it. Replacement hose of this kind can be adapted to fit older cleaners. There are quite a number of shops who do this kind of work exclusively. Take the end fittings of your original hose to one of these shops, and they can put on any desired length of the new-type hose which will last a lot longer.

12

Electric Sewing Machines

The electric sewing machine is a pretty simple device, *electrically.* A small motor is mounted on one end of the body, and it drives the machine through a rubber belt. It is a variable-speed brush-type motor. The speed is controlled by a foot-operated rheostat which is simply a series resistance to vary the voltage applied to the motor. It opens the circuit when the pedal is fully released, so that it also serves as an on-off switch.

For obvious reasons, we are not going to recommend making any mechanical repairs to the *insides* of these machines. This demands a real expert who understands the working parts and has a great assortment of special tools. So, while electrical repair can be made without too much trouble since all of the working parts are outside, we will deal only with the electrical operation. Fig. 12-1 shows the electrical parts of a sewing machine, less the foot switch. The motor is mounted on the end of the body, on an attached bracket. Note that this is slotted in order to allow for adjustment of belt tension. In this model, the small three-terminal block is mounted on the same bracket, under the motor. The wires from the motor and the built-in light fasten to this. A plastic cover slips over the wires, so that all electrical connections are completely covered while the machine is in use.

Fig. 12-2 shows the electrical circuit of the machine. This is a brush-type motor, usually called a "universal-wound" type; the synchronous motors will not work in this kind of application. The speed is controlled by varying the voltage, and you cannot do this with the

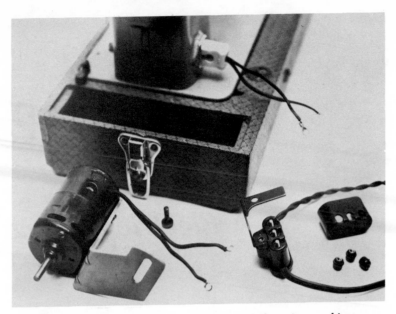

Fig. 12-1. The electrical portion of a typical sewing machine.

synchronous types. Notice that the light is hooked directly across the line at all times. If it were connected across the motor terminals, it would dim or brighten as the speed of the motor is changed, and go out entirely when the foot switch is pressed.

Fig. 12-3 shows the bottom view of the speed-control rheostat unit. In this model the resistance wires are completely enclosed in a hard, lavalike insulator. The contact is made by a slider on the other side, not visible here. The wires fasten to two terminal screws, near the bottom. The pedal, on the other (top) side, moves the rod back and forth to change the resistance. The heavy spring at the

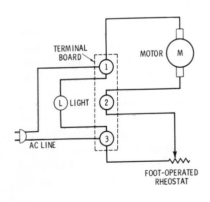

Fig. 12-2. The electrical circuit of the sewing machine.

bottom is the pedal-return spring. The hook-shaped bracket on the rod is a shorting device; when the pedal is pushed all the way down, it shorts the two wires by means of the two small leaf switches. This takes all of the resistance out of the circuit and lets the motor run

Fig. 12-3. Interior view of the foot-control switch.

full speed. The resistance is built so that the slider goes completely off when the pedal is all the way up; this opens the circuit and stops the motor.

Some of these control units will have exposed-wire–type resistance elements. The sliders will then be on the bottom side, riding over the wire. If they develop poor contact, sparking, etc., the wire can be cleaned, and the ends of the contact arms bent slightly to be sure that they make a good firm contact with the wires at all places when they move. *Do not* work on this type (or any of them, for that matter) with the machine plugged in; there are always exposed wires that can give you a severe shock.

ELECTRICAL TROUBLES

Most of the electrical troubles found in these machines will generally be simple ones; broken wires, worn brushes in the motors, and loose connections on the foot-control switch. Keep a close watch on the condition of the a-c cord and wires between the switch and the motor. If you see any sign of frayed insulation or if the cord is old, replace it at once. Since they are used among piles of loose cloth, patterns, and so on, a short circuit between the wires can cause a serious "flash fire." Do not take chances, or use slipshod methods of repair, like taping up bad places; put on a new wire.

If the motor will not run at all, but the light burns, check the speed control. Try pushing it all the way down; this should short out the resistance element and make the motor run full-speed. As a last resort, you can take off one of the *control* wires and fasten it to the other one, thus shorting the speed control completely, and letting the motor run. In both sealed-element and open-wire–type controls, the best repair is a new resistance element. The sealed units cannot be taken apart, and the open-wire types are made with resistance wire, which cannot be soldered. Many of these use riveted connections. If one of these is loose, take the rivet out completely, by grinding or filing one end, and put a small bolt and nut in its place. Use two flat washers with the wires pinched between them, and always use a lockwasher under the nut, so that the bolt will not come loose. You can make connections to resistance wire in this way, if you have to, when replacing an open-wire element.

If shorting the speed control entirely will not make the motor hum, there is an open circuit somewhere inside the motor itself. The most likely trouble is a worn brush or one that has stuck in its holder so that it is not touching the commutator surface. The brushes on almost all of these motors can be replaced without even taking the motor off the bracket. You will find two small plastic screw caps in the end bell; unscrew these, and the brushes should pop out into your hand. Check them for length; these little motors use pretty short brushes at best, usually about ½ inch long. If they are worn to less than about ¼ inch, put in new ones. By pulling on the end of the spring, make sure that the brush can slide in and out of the holder very freely. There must be no binding at all. If a new brush is tight, rub it on a piece of fine sandpaper held on the bench until it will slide freely in and out.

If brushes start to wear or get too short, you will notice a very loud sputtering as the motor runs. There will also be flashes of vivid blue light coming from the air holes in the motor (and a very loud noise in any radios or television sets). This is always a sign of trouble, and it should be checked as soon as it shows up. A jammed brush can cause such heavy arcing that a perfectly good commutator can be ruined in only a short time. At the least, it can save you from tearing the motor down to clean a very dirty commutator.

Motors seem to be very much the same size and type on all makes. They are held together by two long bolts through the end bells; you can see the screw head on one end and a nut on the other. To take one apart, disconnect the wires, and remove the brushes. Now take out the two long bolts. You can usually pull the end bell off the

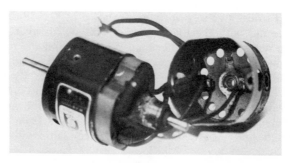

Fig. 12-4. Sewing machine motor with one housing end removed.

motor by twisting it gently in your hands. If it is stuck tightly, look for the crack between the end bell and frame. Insert the blade of a small screwdriver in the crack and pry first on one side then the other. Do not use too much force—you can bend the thin sheet-metal of the end bell and make it hard to get a snug fit when you put it back together. Fig. 12-4 shows a motor with one end bell loosened up.

Most of the motor housing will not come apart entirely. As you can see, the brush holders are mounted on the end bell and connected to the field coils with insulated wires. Be careful when you are taking this end bell off so that you do not accidentally break these wires. They are not too long. The motor must be taken down this far in order to clean the commutator, since you cannot get at it at all with the motor assembled. Smooth it off with a thin strip of fine sandpaper until it is shiny again. The brushes connect with the field coils. Most of these motors use the electrical circuit of Fig. 12-5. Note that one field coil is on either side of the armature. This is done mainly to avoid as much radio interference as possible. The field coils act as "chokes" to keep the brush arcs from getting back into the a-c line and into radios, etc.

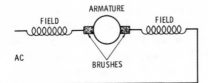

Fig. 12-5. Electric circuit of a sewing-machine motor.

While most mounting bolts go all the way through the housing or case, some will be made like the one in Fig. 12-4. Here, the nuts are on small brackets stamped out of the other end bell. These can be hard to get to, unless you have a set of the miniature box-end wrenches sold in auto-supply stores as "ignition wrenches." However, you can use two screwdrivers as shown in Fig. 12-6 by prying against the nut with the blade of one. This will hold it while you loosen the screw with the other one. When you put the motor back together, be sure that all wires are clear, so that they do not pinch between the end bell and frame, jam the commutator, etc. A pinched wire could cause a short to the body of the motor and create a bad shock hazard to the user. To make sure, hook up the motor, turn it on (keeping *out* of contact with it), and check from the motor frame to a ground with the test lamp. The neon lamp will do for this test.

Also, notice that the motor is not round but has two flat sides. As you can see in Fig. 12-4, one of these sides has two threaded holes for attaching the mounting brackets. Be sure that the end bell is not reversed; if so, you will cover up one of the house. Also, the wires to the brush holders will probably be too short, pulled across the armature, jamming it. There are oil holes in the end bells, just above the bearings. Felt wicks are usually provided inside the end bell so that the bearings will not run dry. Put about one or two drops of oil in each hole if they seem to be dry Do not use too much, for

Fig. 12-6. A method of removing motor-housing bolts.

here again we could get an oil drip on the fabric being sewed, and thus get into deep trouble.

If the motor groans or refuses to run but makes a loud humming noise, stop the machine, take the belt off, and spin the motor pulley with your fingers. If you can feel it dragging, oil it lightly and spin it again. Then try it without the belt, a "no-load" condition. If it starts immediately and runs up to full speed without making a lot of arcing or any other kind of noise except for a "happy whir," it is probably in operating condition. However, if it sparks heavily or still hums, even though the pulley spins freely, you probably have an open armature or field coil, or a shorted armature. The motor will have to be rebuilt or replaced. Although this depends on the availability of a good motor-rewinder in your area, it is often cheaper to buy a new armature or a new motor than to have these tiny armatures rewound. They are much harder to rewind than a large-size motor.

DRIVE BELTS AND CLUTCHES

Although drive belts and clutches are not strictly electrical, still they are parts of the machine that are "outside" and comparatively easy to fix. The machines are driven by a small rubber belt. The original models used a round belt, perhaps in memory of the round leather belts used on the foot-powered machines. Later ones use a belt that is exactly like the V-belts used on cars, but considerably smaller. A small pulley on the motor shaft and a V-groove in the large handwheel on the end of the machine do the driving. V-belts don't need as much tension as round ones because of their design; the belt jams in the walls of the groove and grips it very tightly. If the belt gets too loose to pull the machine without slipping, loosen the motor mounting bolts and let it drop slightly until the belt tightens up. The proper belt tension should be just enough so that you can feel a little bit of slack when you pull straight out on the belt, between pulleys.

If a belt gets oil or grease on its inner surface, it can slip. Wipe it clean and then wipe it with a cloth dampened with lighter fluid, to remove as much oil as possible. Always leave the belt surface as dry as possible for maximum "grip." Wipe the grooves in both pulleys with a cloth moistened with lighter fluid. All machines have a clutch which is used to disconnect the large handwheel from the mechanism. This is done so that the big wheel can be used to rewind bobbins, etc. by means of a small rubber tire on the bobbin winder, which contacts the front part of the handwheel without moving the needle and other parts. This is operated by a smaller disc or wheel on the end of the main drive shaft. To loosen the clutch, hold the handwheel and turn the small disc about ¼ turn counterclockwise. Now the handwheel should turn freely without moving the needle.

The clutch couples the two wheels by means of a specially shaped disc mounted between them. The end of the main drive shaft has a wide slot, and lugs on the side of the clutch disc engage the wheels.

Fig. 12-7. Removing setscrew to adjust
clutch mechanism.

The small disc on the outside engages the inner disc by means of a small setscrew visible in the end of the disc. To adjust the clutch, this screw can sometimes be tightened or loosened. Hold the handwheel with one hand and turn the setscrew with the other, as shown in Fig. 12-7.

In most makes, this set screw should be tight, but in a few it is adjustable. If the clutch jams, take the setscrew out and unscrew the disc from the end of the drive shaft, turning it counterclockwise. Examine the inner disc to see if it jammed, corroded, or needs oil. This type of clutch can use just a little bit of oil, but once again, take it easy. If too much oil is used, it will drip out.

13

Electric Timers and Clocks

You will find electric clocks on many appliances, such as washers, dryers, and others which go through cycles. The electric clock is used for switching cycles on or off at preset intervals. Electric ranges, for example, use clocks to turn oven or burners on or off at any hour you want. Besides this, there are even a few that are used for their original purpose—keeping time.

An electric clock or timer is generally a simple device *electrically*. Mechanically, they are pretty complex, but in the electrical department they consist of just one small coil of wire. This is sealed up in a tight housing. The current through the coil causes a very light aluminum disc to turn. This drives a very small pinion gear, and this, in turn drives the "clockworks" through a very complicated system of reduction gears. This is the very simplest synchronous electric motor, which runs at a speed set by the frequency of the a-c power supply.

If lightning hits near your house, the fine wire of the coil may be burnt out by the sudden heavy surge of current. In almost all clocks like this, the motor-coil unit is replaceable. Fig. 13-1 shows a unit removed from the case. The motor coil is the round black object. It is held to the chassis by the two very small screws seen on the two small flanges at the sides of the case. Fig. 13-2 shows the motor taken off the chassis. The small pinion gear can be seen on the motor unit. The small screwdriver lying nearby is a special screw-holding type, almost a necessity when trying to put the tiny screws back in the tight places found on most clock motors.

The coil is easy to test. Take the movement out of the case. Plug it in and look at the back of the motor unit. There is always a small hole where you can see the aluminum disc. Since this is perforated, you can tell whether it is turning or not when you hook up the clock to the a-c line. In this one, the view hole is at the center. In other models, it may be near the outside rim. If the disc is turning, the motor is operating; if it is not, then the motor coil may be open. Check with the neon tester or test lamp to make sure that there is power at the clock wire terminals. If there is power, and the disc is not moving, the diagnosis is complete: The motor is bad. You can get replacement motor units at appliance stores, electrical supply stores, etc. Copy the make and model-number information from the clock unit. This will be stamped on the clock case or on a small metal plate fastened to it somewhere. Take the old motor unit along, so that you will be sure to get the right size and shape. While they are all alike electrically, no two of them are duplicates physically; they may have different numbers of teeth on the pinion, etc. Make sure that you have an *exact* duplicate, or it will not work.

The actual replacement is simple; just fit the new unit into the place where the old one was. Make sure that the pinion engages the

Fig. 13-1. Electric clock with detachable motor unit.

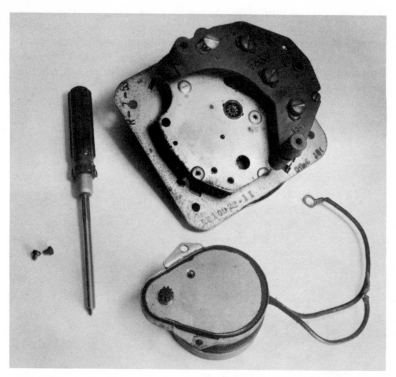

Fig. 13-2. Electric clock unit removed from gear assembly.

teeth of the driven gear, and never force it into place. When you get it installed properly, it will slip into position very easily. Be sure that the flanges of the case are down flat on the chassis and that screw holes are lined up, etc. With the screw-holding screwdriver, put the screws back, and tighten them. If you don't have one of these handy gadgets, you can sometimes put a tiny bit of wax or gum on the tip of the blade, and "stick" the screw to this. It will usually hold long enough to help you get the screw in place. If all else fails, try placing the screw in the hole with a pair of tweezers, and then starting it with the screwdriver.

The wires will be hooked up to a "terminal board" on the clock chassis, as you can see at the top of Fig. 13-2. Make up a rough sketch of the wires as they were originally connected, *before* disconnecting any of them. Note wire size, color, or any kind of distinguishing feature. If they should be all of the same color, take small pieces of white surgical tape and wrap it around the end of each wire. Write a number, or any other identification, on this with a ball point pen. When you replace the wires, make sure that each

115

is on the original terminal and that they are all tight. Also, be sure that the insulation on each wire is tight up against the terminal lugs. Never leave bare places on the insulation which might let two wires touch each other, or touch the metal frame of the clock. If necessary, tape these places so that there will never be a chance of them making electrical contact.

Fig. 13-3. An electric clock with different mounting brackets.

Fig. 13-3 shows another clock, exactly like the first but built quite a bit differently. Note the heavy terminal board. This is provided with heavy flaps of "fish-paper" which fold over the terminals when the wiring is installed, for added protection against possible short circuits. In this one, the motor is underneath, as it lies, but you can always identify it. It is the only section which has two wires going to it. The same type of mounting is used: two small screws on the sides of the motor case. These are on the bottom in this photo.

Fig. 13-4 shows a replacement motor unit for still another make of clock; note the similarity of construction, wires, pinion gear, etc. There is one thing you will find on a lot of these units, particularly if they are used as timers on electric ranges: There will be a heavy-duty switch mounted on the clock mechanism. Such a switch is part of the terminal board assembly in the clock unit shown in Fig. 13-3, but the shaft is underneath and not visible. This is generally hooked up as a "master switch"; in other words, if it is not in the *on* position, nothing can work. This has caused some confusion among users. If

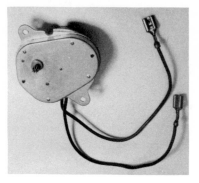

Fig. 13-4. Various styles and shapes of electric clock motors.

this switch happens to be knocked into the *off* position when cleaning, etc., the stove will be dead without apparent cause. This switch will have three positions: "OFF," "MANUAL," and "AUTO" (automatic). The actual names vary between different makes, of course, but these three functions are always there. To control the range with the regular knobs on each unit, the switch must be in the manual position. To make the automatic timing feature work properly, the switch must be in the *auto* position. In *off* position, the complete unit is disconnected. This has caused many unnecessary service calls, so be sure to check it before sending for a repairman. As a last resort, read the instruction book that comes with every one of these units.

14

Three-Way Lamps

Three-way lamps are found in almost all homes, in one version or another. They can be table or floor lamps with two or more bulbs which can be switched on one at a time, or all at once. A standard sequence for these would be "1," "2," "both," and then off. Some versions use a three-way bulb, with 100-200-300—watt filaments. Other versions use single bulbs and a selector switch as shown in Fig. 14-1.

To find the trouble, make sure that all bulbs are good; this is easy—just screw a known-good bulb into the suspected socket. If it is a bad switch, one particular bulb will refuse to light or light

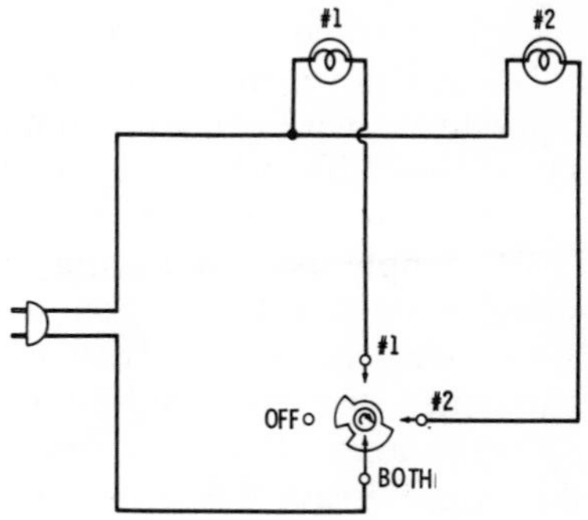

Fig. 14-1. Diagram illustrating a three-way switch.

every other time the switch is turned to that position. Bad switches will usually become very noisy; the bulb will flicker on and off and you will hear a loud noise in the radio or television. The switches themselves are not too easy to repair. A bad contact is usually burned up from long use, and in any case the construction of the switch makes it very difficult to take apart and put back together. The best way is to install a new switch which is inexpensive, and you will get much better service.

Fig. 14-2. A typical three-way lamp with the selector switch exposed.

To repair one of these, take the switch housing apart. Fig. 14-2 shows a typical lamp, opened and ready for checking. There will be two or three small screws holding it together. The wires will be tucked down inside the body of the lamp. Pull them up and separate the wires so that you can see which ones go to the switch. They should be fastened together with wirenuts. These are solderless connectors made especially for this kind of work. To take one apart, simply hold the wires near the wirenut and unscrew it, going counterclockwise. You will see that the ends of the wires are twisted together; untwist them and pull them apart. You will also notice that one wire from the line cord goes to the wires going up to the lamps. This is the *common* wire, and it does not go through the switch. Leave this alone; you do not have to bother it. Take all of the switch wires loose, and unscrew the knurled nut holding the switch on the lamp. Use a pair of small gas-pliers to loosen the nut and remove the old switch.

You can get replacement switches at any electrical-appliance dealer's store. If you have any doubt, take the old switch with you so that you will be sure to get one with the right number of positions, etc. Put the new switch in, and tighten it well, so that the body of the switch will not turn when you turn the lamp on and off. Bring the wire leads up and out so that you can get at them to make the connections. To make this kind of connection, strip the insulation about ¼ inch from the ends of the wires. Twist the strands clockwise. The wires on the new switch will already be stripped ready to hook up. The other wires should be clipped off neatly to make new ends, in order to get the best connection.

Hold the wires together, going the same way, and twist the ends clockwise a couple of times. Put the open end of the wirenut over the ends of the wires, and tighten it by turning it clockwise until you feel it tighten up. Be very sure that the insulation of the wires go up into the end of the wirenut so that there are no bare wires showing at all. You need only about ¼ inch of bare wire to make this connection. If you have more than this, clip the end off with a pair of cutters.

Make up the other connections in the same way, and plug the lamp in and check it. Be sure that you have good bulbs. Ordinarily, you will have it hooked up right. The case of the new switch will be marked "L" for *line*, "1" and "2" for the two lamps. Be sure that the wire from the line cord goes to the L wire on the switch, and the others can go to either one. If this should be a pole lamp, with three separate bulbs, they originally lit up from the top down, etc. You may have to change one or two of the bulb wires to get it back in the original order. On the two-lamp units, it does not make a great deal of difference which is "1" or "2."

If your lamp has the solid-metal shades, you may have trouble with the lamp sockets overheating. If there is not enough ventilation or oversize bulbs are used, the sockets or wiring can suffer from heat deterioration. They are not hard to replace; each socket is held by a knurled nut at the top, like the switch. Always use replacement sockets made out of ceramic or heat-resistant plastic. Watch out for wires with rubber insulation. If it is old and has been over-heated, the insulation will crack and fall off as the lamp is moved around. This can cause a dangerous short circuit, blowing the fuse. Also, one of the wires may contact the base of the lamp which could cause a fatal electric shock.

When you are working on these lamps, always check the condition of the wiring. If it is old, frayed, or the insulation is very brittle, do not take any chances. Replace all wiring with new wires and be sure to use wire with asbestos or a fiberglass-type insulation. Get stranded wire, so that it will hold up under constant bending and flexing which it will get when the lamp is moved around and adjusted.

15

Hedge Trimmers

Electric hedge trimmers come in all sizes, from the heavy-duty models intended for park use down to lighter home-types. Fig. 15-1 shows a heavy-duty model, powered by a good-sized electric motor. This is a rotary cutter and its operation is like that of a chain saw. The cutting teeth are connected into an endless chain, and they travel in a groove around the fixed blade.

The chain of teeth is driven by a gear, which in turn is driven by a worm gear on the end of the motor shaft. This is enclosed in a sealed gearbox. Fig. 15-2 shows this box with the cover removed so that you can see the heavy bronze pinion. This gearbox should always be kept filled with a high-viscosity grease. The pinion is made of bronze for longer life and quieter running. The gearbox cover is held in place by four small screws. A gasket is used to keep in the grease. When the cover is taken off and replaced, check the

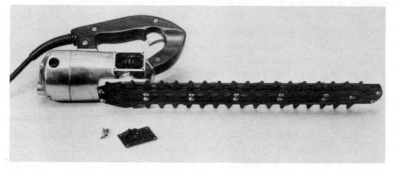

Fig. 15-1. Heavy-duty hedge trimmers.

condition of the gasket so that the grease will not leak out when the machine gets hot during long use.

The motor brushes are accessible from outside. Insulated caps on either side cover the brush holders. To check the brushes, unscrew the caps and pull the brushes out by the springs. Be careful; the brush springs used on this kind of motor are heavy, and the cap

Fig. 15-2. Hedge trimmer with gear box cover removed.

may be flipped off and lost, especially if this is done outdoors. Cover the cap with your other hand so that it cannot escape. Fig. 15-3 shows a good brush, which is at least ¾ inch long and very smooth and shiny on the commutator. The brush cap is lying on the motor.

The switch on this unit is actuated by a trigger. The switch itself is inside the handle. This is made in two pieces, held together by *Phillips* screws, as you can see in Fig. 15-2. To remove the switch, remove these screws and pull the handle apart. In most cases, one half of the handle will be fastened to the motor housing, and the other half will come off when the screws are taken out. The switch body and trigger fit into slots on the inside of the handle.

Fig. 15-4 shows a lighter-duty model, which is powered by an electric drill. The drive gears are in the small box just in front of

124

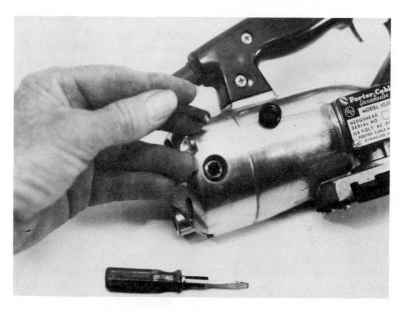

Fig. 15-3. Checking the motor brushes for wear.

the drill chuck. A ¼-inch shaft comes out of the box and is chucked into the drill. The body of the drill is clamped to the handle with a metal strap. This type uses a reciprocating motion. The cutting teeth are on a movable bar. The shaft drives a small pinion gear,

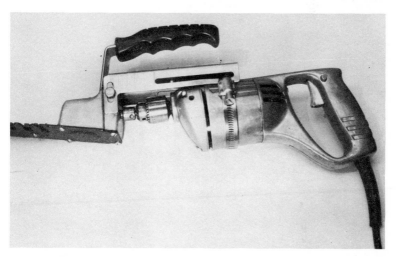

Fig. 15-4. Hedge trimmers powered by a ¼-inch electric drill.

which in turn drives a larger bevel gear. On the other side of this is a stud fitting into a slot in the end of the movable blade. As the bevel gear turns, this stud pulls the movable blade back and forth to give the reciprocating motion. Four screws hold the gearbox to the body of the unit.

To sharpen either of these, set the mechanism so that the cutting edges of the moving teeth fall into the notches in the fixed blade. They can then be smoothed off and sharpened with a small, narrow, flat file. This will do very well for "touchup" sharpening, but if the blade is very dull, it will probably have to be taken apart and resharpened on a special machine. Whenever you are working on these machines, be certain that the line plug is pulled; they are dangerous. To reduce wear on gears, blade, and teeth, be sure that they are well oiled at all times. A heavy-bodied oil is best; it will stay on the blades and not be thrown off. Most cutters have several oil holes in the blades so that oil can get to all moving parts.

Keep a sharp eye on the line cord when you are using this kind of machine. It is possible to make a sharp turn and gather up the cord as you go—into the cutting blades, that is. Never use this kind of machine when it is raining or when the ground is very wet. There is always the chance of an internal short circuit which could cause a fatal shock. All of these should be equipped with three-conductor line cords. The third wire is connected to the body of the unit, and then well-grounded at the outlet. If one of the hot wires should contact the body, the current will go to ground instead of *to you*. It will blow a fuse or trip a circuit breaker, but that's better than getting a severe shock.

Index